ALASKA
on the Fly
by
Dan Heiner

**Come Along with Alaska Outdoor Writer Dan Heiner
As He Fly Fishes For Alaska's Rainbow Trout
and Other Trophy Sport Fish Species**

**FLY FISHING
BRISTOL BAY • WESTERN ALASKA
SOUTHCENTRAL ALASKA**

ISBN 0-9637407-1-7

-Manufactured in the United States of America-

Type Font: Times

Word Processing Assistance: David Stark

Photo Scans: TimeFrame

Layout/Format: Publication Consultants

Title Credit: John Swett

Illustrations by: Karol Fogel

Dan Heiner's Articles Have Appeared In:

Flyfishing magazine

Safari magazine

Alaska Outdoors magazine

Alaska Outdoor Times

THIS IS HIS FIRST BOOK

ISBN 0-9637407-1-7

CONTENTS

CONTENTS

•DEDICATION•

ALASKA *on the Fly©* is dedicated to my father, Daniel P. Heiner. I couldn't begin to thank my Dad enough for sharing his time with me in the outdoors over the years. I'm always anxious for summer to arrive so that I may spend time with him again fishing Alaska. My Dad has always been my best friend and he remains my favorite fishing partner.

Thanks must go to my wife, Anne, for understanding my desires of experiencing Alaska, and the time and travel it requires.

I'd also like to extend a special note of thanks to *Great Alaska Fish Camp* guide, Steve Fickes, who's fly fishing demonstration a few years ago served to renew my enthusiasm for the joys of catching and releasing wild trout on tiny flies, a sport my father taught me when I was a teenager. Steve will be pleased to know that since that day I have gone on to fish approximately half of Alaska's eighty-odd premier rivers. It goes without saying that I'm looking forward to experiencing all I can of the others, too.

A very special thanks must go to Evan E. Swensen, Editor & Publisher of A*laska Outdoors* magazine and *Alaska Outdoor Times*. Evan saw to it that I was able to experience this land called Alaska in a way that otherwise never would have been possible. I shall always be grateful to Evan for pointing me in the direction of my Alaska dream.

Author's father, Daniel P. Heiner and Fish River guide take a closeup look at a northern pike.

Finally, this book is dedicated to those fly fishermen who release rainbow trout, char, and grayling ...to live....to fight another day.

•FOREWORD•

by Raymond F. "Sonny" Petersen
Owner, Katmailand, Inc.
'Angler's Paradise'
Kulik, Grosvenor, and Brooks Lodges

O ver the past several years I've come to know Dan Heiner through his visits to our lodges at Katmai: *Brooks and Kulik*. In early June, Dan can usually be found fly fishing Brooks River for rainbows during the opener. In July he'll stop by again to fish and photograph bears at Brooks River Falls. Then, in late August or early September, Dan will fish dry flies for rainbows at our premiere Kulik Lodge."

It pleases me that Dan has taken the time to write **ALASKA** *on the Fly*. I know he has personally experienced much of Alaska's best fly fishing, and his desire for sharing Alaska's fishing with others is obvious.

What pleases me most, however, are the subjects Dan has chosen to discuss in his book. Visitors need to understand How to Select a Lodge, what the best times to fish for Alaska's sport fish species are, and things like, 'How to Release Fish, alive and unharmed. Topics such as, 'Learning To Fly Fish,' 'Choosing the Right Equipment,' and 'How To Select A River' are important, too.

'**ALASKA** *on the Fly*' should do well to inform Alaska's visitors about many of the details regarding Alaska's fishing, just as it should be a help to them in learning the wide range of fishing opportunities that exist in The Last Frontier.

I can only hope that those who read this book will feel the excitement that comes with Alaska's fly fishing, and will want to experience it personally."

Raymond F. "Sonny" Petersen
May 1993

• ACKNOWLEDGMENTS •

I 'm not sure I could begin to thank all the individuals who've assisted me in my fly fishing travels across Alaska over the years without inadvertently omitting someone. Consequently, I'll simply say - to Owners, Managers, Assistants, Guides, Pilots, Cooks, and to all others who have helped me...a very sincere *Thank You*. I am aware of the sacrifices you have made to assist me in experiencing Alaska's best. This book is but one of the ways I can begin to repay my debt of gratitude to each of you.

You and I both know who you are.

-Dan Heiner

•ABOUT THIS BOOK•

For nearly a decade, now, it has been the author's privilege to experience, photograph, and write about many of Alaska's sport fishing lodges in the pages of *Alaska Outdoors* magazine and *Alaska Outdoor Times* . During this time Dan has enjoyed the opportunity of getting to know many of Alaska's lodge owners and their staff members personally. ALASKA *on the Fly©* is an invitation to readers to 'Come Along' with Dan Heiner as he relives many of his favorite Alaska fly fishing experiences.

"ALASKA *on the Fly©* was written primarily with the 'would-be' Alaska fly fisher in mind. Those who already know some of Alaska's premier fisheries

Come along with Dan as he fly fishes many of Alaska's best rivers.

will find this book to be an overview of the excitement that comes with experiencing and fly fishing The Great Land's best lakes and rivers.

ALASKA *on the Fly©* was not written under the pretense of being an all-encompassing, statewide treatise on either the technical, the 'How To,' or the scientific aspects of Alaska's fishing and its species. Rather, what it is, hopefully, is a mirror to the enjoyment that is waiting to be experienced at Alaska's best lakes and rivers.

The main area of focus of this book is the fly fishing to be found in Bristol Bay, Southcentral Alaska, and Western Alaska. Special attention is paid in this book to the fly fishing for Alaska's wild rainbow trout.

As Field Editor, and then, later, as Managing Field Editor of *Alaska Outdoors* magazine and *Alaska Outdoor Times*, I have been privileged to experience many of Alaska's best fisheries. This book is a reflection of these experiences.

ALASKA *on the Fly©* might not answer *all* of the questions a potential angler will have about Alaska's fly fishing, but it should assist in helping him to better discern those answers for himself. An attempt has been made to write this book in a casual, personal manner, one which, hopefully, will make the reading more enjoyable.

Many references to specific individuals, areas, rivers, lakes, and fishing lodges** are given in this book in order to present an accurate, realistic picture of modern day Alaska. It is hoped readers will be able to get a more realistic feel of 'real Alaska' by mentioning many of the real participants. It is hoped that **ALASKA** *on the Fly*© will cause fishermen of all ages and genders to want to experience the many fishing opportunities Alaska offers.

For those who will only dream of doing so, it is hoped this book will provide the spark of adventure that dwells in the hearts of fly fishermen everywhere. And, for those who are destined to experience Alaska, personally, hopefully this book will help prepare you for your visit."

**Because of the ever-changing nature of the fishing lodge business, readers should be aware that the lodges, individuals, and services listed herein are subject to change. All blame, of course, rests with the myriad of intangibles intrinsic to the fishing business, itself. These intangibles are sometimes magnified in Alaska, a state one-fifth the size of the entire lower 48 United States.

•TRIBUTE TO MIKE HERSHBERGER•

H Mike Hershberger was a fly fisher's fly fisher, one of Alaska's most experienced anglers. A member of The Hardy Fly Fishing Hall of Fame, Mike was, above all an Alaskan character who loved to fly fish. Anybody who knew Mike knew a man who loved and lived his passion: *fly fishing.*

Those of us who knew Mike well, either through visiting him at his fly shop in Anchorage or by fishing along side him at Alaska's premier rivers, will long remember his colorful personality.

I never knew anyone who could handle a fly rod as efficiently or present a dry fly as gracefully or accurately as Mike Hershberger. Few individuals I've known have experienced as many Alaska's rivers as Mike Hershberger.

H. Mike Hershberger, and his annual 'Fly Fishing Seminar' held at Brooks River in June of each year will be sorely missed.

Mike Hershberger and Jim Salisbury discuss fly fishing while at Brooks River during 'Hershberger Fly Fishing Seminar.'

9

BECOMING
A FLY FISHER

O ne of the things that never ceases to amaze me is the 'difficulty factor' many people place on the *"Art of Fly Fishing."* Over the years I've had numerous 'hardware' fishermen say things like, "...I don't think I could *ever* learn all those difficult fly fishing casts and fancy moves you guys make. Whipping your fly lines around and all like you do... How in the world do you ever keep everything from getting tangled?"

Like I say, I've always had a hard time dealing with these unwarranted accolades. Some individuals insist on turning fly fishers into semi-gods, whether they deserve it, or not.

Doesn't everybody know?

...almost anyone can learn to fly fish.

I'm willing to bet that any person possessing an arm and a minimal amount of coordination can learn to cast a fly line and catch fish. The thing to remember is, the fish (themselves) don't know if a fly has been cast by a beginner or by an expert with years of experience. Chances are, if the offering looks decent, the fish will come for the fly, regardless.

Fish On!

If someone were to say to me, " I'd like you to teach me to fly fish," I'd probably reply something like, "Great. Come on over to the yard for a half hour and I'll teach you everything I know."

I'd mean it, too.

It might sound like I'm trying to be coy—but I'm not. It's the simple truth. All I might know that a non-fly fisher might *not* is that fish are usually hungry and often rush to a variety of flies. Consequently.... it's fun catching them on a fly rod. It's a little like the private bushpilot I met once (I've forgotten his name) who wouldn't admit he was supposed to have a pilot's license before he began flying his Super Cub through some of Alaska's tallest mountain ranges. In the classic tradition, he learned to fly as many have learned to fly fish — by getting out and doing it.

Experience is a great teacher.

I'm willing to bet I can teach almost anyone to cast a fly line, and here is how I'd go about it:

(1) Imagine you're standing on a large, wide-open lawn with no obstacles around you for a hundred yards in any direction. In your 'rod' hand you hold a

9-foot, 6-weight fly rod. For your convenience, the rod is already strung-up with an easy-to-see, yellow, 6-weight floating weight-forward fly line. Installed on the rod, near the base of your 'rod hand' is a small, simple fly reel - an instrument used primarily for the purpose of holding additional amounts of fly line and backing. For now, you can forget about the reel while we concentrate solely on casting.

Let's assume that approximately 15 yards of yellow fly line are lying on the lawn in front of you. Don't worry about connecting a leader or "tippet"

With the basics of fly casting you can fish any water in Alaska. This rainbow was taken on a dry fly while fishing from Kulik Lodge.

to the end of the fly line just yet - We'll cover all that in a few minutes.

(2) To gain an understanding of the principle called 'loading the rod,' imagine a long, vertical antenna installed on an automobile's fender. Tied to the end of the antenna is a long, red ribbon. When the car moves down the highway the red ribbon flows to the rear of the antenna, flapping horizontally in the breeze as the car travels. The faster the car travels, the more the red ribbon bends (or loads) the tip top of the antenna. Now, imagine pulling at the end of the red ribbon until you 'load' it, and then let go of the ribbon. The reflex action of the antenna (rod) will send the ribbon in the opposite direction.

The key things to remember in this simple scenario are: (A) the red ribbon flows *horizontal* to the ground while the car moves and becomes tightly suspended, and (B) the base of the antenna (where it is mounted on the car's fender) *does not* bend much. Most of the bend in the antenna is further up the shaft, and it bends more as additional pressure is exerted against it. In fly casting, this bending is referred to as, "loading the rod.' The base of the rod (or antenna) doesn't bend in the caster's hand past the "11:00 Position or the 1:00 Position on 'the clock.'"

In fly casting, it's the actual weight of the fly line, itself, that bends, or 'loads' the fly rod. A 6-weight fly line is specifically designed (in weight) to match with a 6-weight rod, etc. Fly rods and fly lines are manufactured in sizes 1 (light) to size 15 (heavy). The size of fly rod/line 'tool' you select will vary for the different species you'll fish for.

The simple scenario of the automobile's antenna describes the two secrets of casting a fly line. One of the keys is keeping slack out of the cast. The only other thing a would-be-fly fisher needs to remember is....Don't bend the wrist past 11:00 or 1:00 on the 'clock,' and....WAIT until the backcast tightens horizontally..... before beginning the forward cast ...and WAIT until the forward cast tightens horizontally before beginning the backcast ....and WAIT.....until..

The movement of the wrist in the casting action is almost negligible. It's the...WAIT...

> *"Fly Fishing is a sport created for man's enjoyment. Anybody who tries to make it scientific, or too much more than this has missed the point. Entirely."*
> *Dan Heiner*

that differentiates the great fly casters from the run of the mill. It's all in the timing, which allows the weight of the line, *itself,* to "load' the fly rod tip. WAIT until the fly line tightens in one direction before beginning it in the other direction. This 'back and forth' motion, while fishing, is referred to as, "False Casting," which either allows a dry fly fisher to *dry* his fly before 'presenting' it again on the water, or it allows a fishermen to gradually change the direction of his cast.

Don't get in the habit of false casting too much, however. There's an old saying regarding 'false casting' that still applies today; "You're not fishing for OWLS, you're fishing for fish, so keep your fly on the water, *Not in the Air!"*

What you're doing when you're casting a fly line, in reality, is allowing the actual WEIGHT of the fly line to "LOAD" the rod tip so it is forced to spring (itself) back in the opposite direction. Back, forth, back, forth... Once you've applied distance, direction, and energy to the cast you've determined the type of cast you'll be making. Delicate? Punched? Tight? Open? All these things are decided in milliseconds while the fly fisherman scans the waters around him. The way a fly is cast to the water is called, "the Presentation."

The weight of the fly line is important since it must be enough (but not too much) to load the fly rod correctly. This is why light, 'weaker' rods (the 2-weights, 3-weights, 4-weights, etc.) are loaded by lighter lines than are the 10-weights, 11-weights, 12-weights, etc.), which weigh more than lines with smaller numbers. For example, a 6-weight line Will Not load a 9-weight rod sufficiently, no matter how much the angler might want it to. Conversely, a 9-weight line on a 6-weight road would overload the rod, forcing it to bend down right into the grip - and thus lose most of it's "power." Sometimes in windy conditions fly fishers like to throw one-size heavier line to assist in bucking the wind, but one-size larger is about the limit most rods can handle. By the way, there are fifteen fly rod weights available (1 through 15). The 8-weights and 9-weights are those most commonly used for Alaska's diverse tasks of fly fishing.

As opposed to spinfishing, where the lure pulls-out the line by way of momentum, in fly casting it's the weight of the fly line that pulls the fly and the leader along with it - in a trailing "loop." The faster the angler 'punches' a cast, the tighter the loop will be .

Always remember to WAIT (by watching the fly line over your shoulder at all times when first learning)....until the line s-t-r-a-i-g-h-t-e-n-s before begin-ning to power it in the opposite direc-tion after the fly rod has fully "loaded." Learning the steady arm and wrist movement of the backcast is the last 'hurdle' a fly caster usually has to cross before becoming profi-cient - at least proficient enough to go out and enjoy the fly fishing experi-ence.

Now the beginner knows how to cast, and so he also knows just about everything he needs to know. Know-ing how to cast means he's a fly fisher. Why? Because now, all he has to do is attach a fly (either a wet fly or a dry fly will do) to the end of his fly line via a "leader" (which is a tapered piece of monofilament usually about nine feet long) ...and Presto! Flip it out there ....like that ....and....He's fly fishing!

It almost sounds too simple - *and it is.*

Great Alaska Fish Camp *guide, Steve Fickes, with one of several rainbows caught and released at high mountain lake on* Adams dry fly.

Sooner or later (usually sooner) a fish will 'take' the fly, hook itself, and make the beginner look ....*just like* he knew what he was doing all along.

Just like magic! Another fly fisher is born.

Don't worry about all the detailed stuff like fancy knots and things called "tippets" right now. Almost any old knot will suffice at first. Later, you'll learn the improved clinch knot, the needle knot, and, in due time, the blood knot. For right now, concentrate practicing 'false' casting, beginning with moderate amounts of fly line extended.

Another thing about knots: if you're like most fly fishermen who have to wait six or seven months each year before fly fishing season rolls around again, realize you're only normal if you discover you have to refresh your memory about knots 'all over again' next year.

14

Welcome to the club.

Here's the best tip I know regarding becoming a good fly fisher. Spend a good deal of time practicing by lawn casting. Cast tight loops, open loops, fast casts, slow casts....learn them all. Unless you're a natural, like my friend Robby Boyer, you'll discover a great deal of confidence through lawn casting and you'll be able to put your fly line where you want it to go. Casting during 'the real thing' is no different. You'll know what your rod can do and what it can't, and you'll find you'll have fun with the simple sport of fly fishing, rather than becoming frustrated with what is perceived to be a complex "art form."

...and you'll catch fish whether you're an expert or not.

Practice by lawn casting with a floating fly line for an hour or two a day while you're first learning, and, I guarantee, you'll become a good fly fisher. You'll develop a confidence in controlling your fly line (along with your 'tippet,') and, of course, the thing that really matters:

...the *fly* that you've chosen.

Many anglers -like this happy angler from California- visiting Alaska for the first time are surprised at the clearity of Alaska's premier rivers and streams. Learning which rivers are "premier" and which aren't is the key to experiencing "...an Alaska fishing trip of a lifetime."

SELECTING
A RIVER

I probably won't soon forget the first time I ever laid eyes on one of Alaska's most famous rivers. It is a river I had wanted to fish for many years before getting the chance to make my first visit. If readers will forgive me I'll refrain from divulging it's name just now. Suffice it to say, the river appeared much different than what I had expected. It was much deeper and ever so much wider than I had imagined it would be.

Could this be the same river I had heard so much about?

From our seats in the floatplane, Dad and I could look directly over the pilot's shoulder at this river and the surrounding countryside below. Van Hartley, our pilot, banked the deHavilland Beaver in a big, wide, turn, leveling out over the tundra as he lined us up for our river landing.

I could see the river (at least the portion we were over) was much swifter than I had thought it would be. Upstream, at points where it fans out in many 'tributaries,' this river is wadable. But here, at the middle portion where we were, Dad and I found ourselves looking down at an enormous, fast-moving river.

It took me a day or two to get used to it's size...

Upon entering the lodge Dad and I learned the fishing for kings was hot, and even hotter for fresh, incoming chums. Both of these discoveries were good news, but it didn't take me long to realize I'd scheduled our trip at the wrong time of year.

The third week of July is a great time for someone desiring late-run kings, chums, or sockeyes. But, for Dad and me, who were hoping to fish for rainbows, char, and grayling, late August or early September would have been a far better time to make our visit. As an added bonus, August or September would have also provided us with excellent fly fishing for silver salmon.

As things turned out, Dad and I spent four days fishing, both by drifting for salmon from jon boats, and also by wading deep, wide flats, casting 10-weight outfits to large, incoming chums. It was great fun, very exotic and all, and new to both of us. Neither of us had fished for chum salmon exactly in this manner before.

Yet, even though Dad and I developed an appreciation for the 'flavor' of this river, we had been expecting 'Strawberry,' and when the order arrived we were served 'Chocolate.' Like I say, it was all great fun and we made new, long-lasting friends at the lodge, but still, I'd pictured a small, riffly, gravel-bottomed stream in my mind, something quite different from the big, burly river we arrived at.

I learned a good lesson about scheduling fishing trips in Alaska.

(1) Don't expect anything *specifically,* and be pleased with what surprises lie at the end of the rainbow, ...OR,

(2) Do more homework, and know *exactly* what kind of fishing and waters you'll be getting into.

Once an angler arrives at his final Alaska destination, he's pretty-well committed.

I began to wonder how many visiting anglers must come to Alaska each year only to discover similar surprises, or learn that their trip will be just slightly different from what they had origi- *Dr. 'Joe' Chandler from Quinnat Landing fly fishes Alaska's* nally imagined; with *famed American Creek .*

maybe a surprise or two not exactly being part of their "Alaska Dream."

It occurred to me that more than a little research should probably go into planning 'a trip of a lifetime.' Can you imagine the chagrin an angler might feel upon finally arriving in Alaska after a long trip from the east coast or some other faraway place only to discover that the Alaska river he'll be fishing is between 10 and 15 feet deep when he was expecting something entirely wadable? Maybe some people don't mind surprises like this, but some most certainly do, I can assure you.

Because of the diverse conditions the traveler will encounter in The Last Frontier, it's good advice to invest more than a little effort in long distance phone calls and ask specific questions about prospective river/s, lodges, and destinations one might be considering. Speaking directly with a referral who has personally experienced a prospective lodge or fished a particular river being considered can go a long way to providing the traveler with peace of mind about an upcoming trip.

As you can imagine, Alaska offers many different varieties of fly fishing, everything from situations requiring 3-weight outfits for arctic grayling, to those needed to make 90-foot casts for large salmon using 10-weight & 11-weight rods.

That reminds me of another thing to watch out for: many of the advertisements in the magazines that plug Alaska's lodges and guide services look and sound surprisingly alike. Don't go assuming all Alaska fishing trips are equal; *they're not.* They're all very different, believe me.

To prospective visitors I say this: Do your homework. Call each lodge or guide you might be considering service for specific answers and referrals, and don't hesitate to ask what might seem like 'trivial questions.' Visitors have the right to know whether or not they'll have hot and cold running water, for example, or running water, period. And don't go assuming (as some anglers do) that you will have ready access to all fourteen of Alaska's freshwater sport fish species at any one locale. It's a very special river that can offer half of that.

So, go ahead, close your eyes, capture your Alaska dream indelibly in your mind. Then, relate that dream to the lodges you talk with. Chances are, the guy on the other end of the telephone will be a hopeless romantic, too (just like you). *He'd have to be* to actually attempt to make a living guiding dreamers like us.

He'll tell you the best times of year to make your visit — to best optimize your chances of taking the Alaska specie/s you're desiring.

ALASKA'S PREMIER RIVERS, LAKES, & STREAMS

Over the years various lists have been compiled detailing Alaska's top rivers and fisheries. Here is my list—in alphabetical order—according to what I have experienced firsthand and from what I have learned from others. It should be noted that some of Alaska's smaller, premier fisheries have been purposefully omitted from this list - mainly because these unnamed rivers and streams are simply too small to survive an onslaught of fishing pressure.

NUMBER KEY FOR INDIVIDUAL FISH SPECIES:

1 Rainbow Trout	2 Steelhead	3 King Salmon
4 Chum Salmon	5 Sockeye Salmon	6 Silver Salmon
7 Pink Salmon	8 Dolly /Arctic Char	9 Lake 'Trout"
10 Arctic Grayling	11 Sheefish	12 Northern Pike
	13 Cutthroat	

Watershed	Species Number
Agulapok River	1-5-8-10
Agulawok River	1-3-4-5-6-7-8-10
Alagnak River (*Branch)	1-3-4-5-6-7-8-10
Aleknegik Lake	1-3-4-5-6-7-8-10
Alexander Creek	1-3-4-5-6-7-8-10
American Creek	1-5-8
Anchor River	1-2-3-6-7-8
Aniak River	1-3-4-6-7-8-10
Branch River (*Alagnak)	1-3-4-5-6-7-8-10

Alaska *on the Fly*

Brooks River	1-5-6-8-10
Buskin River (Kodiak)	6-7-8
Chatanika River	7-8-10
Chilikadrotna River	1-3-4-5-6-7-8-10
Chuitna River (Chuit)	1-3-6-7-8
Clear Creek	1-3-6-7-10
Copper River	1-5-8-10
Council River	4-6-7-8-10-12
Crescent Lake	1-8-10
Deep Creek	1-2-3-6-7-8
Dream Creek	1-5-8-10
Fish River (White Mountain)	3-4-6-7-8-10-12
Frazer River (Kodiak)	2-5-6-8
Gibralter River	1-5-8
Goodnews River (Western Alaska)	1-3-4-5-6-7-8-10
Gulkana River	1-2-3-5-6-7-8
Holitna River	3-4-6-7-8-10-11
Iliamna River	1-5-8
Kakhonak River	1-5-8-10
Kamishak River	3-4-6-7-8-10
Kanektok River (Western Alaska)	1-3-4-5-6-7-8-10
Karluk River (Kodiak)	2-3-6-7-8
Karta River	2-5-6-7-8-13
Kenai Lake (Outlet)	1-3-5-6-7-8
Kenai River	1-3-5-6-7-8
Kisaralik River	1-3-4-6-7-8-10
Klawock River	1-2-6 + Salt
Kobuk River	4-8-10-11-12
Koktuli River	1-3-4-5-6-7-8-10
Koyuk River	3-4-6-7-8-10
Kukaklek Lake	1-4-5-6-7-8-9-10
Kulik River	1-5-6-8-10
Kvichak River	1-3-4-5-6-7-8-10
Lake Creek	1-3-4-5-6-7-8-10
Lewis Creek	1-3-4-6-7-8
Lake Louise	9-10
Little Willow	3-5-7-10
Minto Flats	10-12
Mulchatna River	1-3-4-5-6-7-8-10
Naknek River	1-3-4-5-6-7-8-10
Naknek Lake	1-3-5-6-7-9-10

Newhalen River	1-5-8-9-10
Nerka Lake	1-5-6-8-9-10-12
Ninilchik River	1-2-3-6-7-8
Nome River	6-7-10
Nonvianuk Lake	1-4-5-6-7-8-9-10
North River	3-4-6-7-8-10
Nushagak River	1-3-4-5-6-7-8-10
Nuyakuk River	1-5-8-10
Nuyakuk Lake	1-5-8-10
Russian River	1-3-5-8
Selawik River (Northern Alaska)	4-8-11-12
Sheep Creek	1-3-6-7-8
Situk River	2-3-6-8
Skilak Lake	1-3-5-6-7-8-9
Swanson River System	1-8
Talachulitna River	1-3-4-5-6-7-8-10
Talkeetna River	1-3-4-6-7-8-10
Talarik Creek, Lower	1-5-8
Theodore	1-3-6-7-8-10
Thorne River (Prince of Wales Island)	2-4-6-7-8-13
Tikchik Lake	1-8-9-10
Tazimina River	1-5-10
Togiak River	1-3-4-5-6-7-8-10
Uganik River (Kodiak)	2-3-5-6-7-8
Ugashik Lakes	5-6-8-10
Unalakleet River	3-4-6-7-8-10
Willow Creek	1-3-6-7-8
Wulik River (Northern Alaska)	4-8-10

Alaska's king salmon can often take an hour or two to land and will test an angler's skill to the limit.

KING SALMON ON A FLY?

It's a funny thing about fly fishermen and Alaska's king salmon. Most anglers can't wait to get the chance to hook one of the behemoth kings. Ironically, a good percentage of those who *do* turn around and swear they never want to subject their bodies to this kind of punishment ever again.

Anyone who's ever 'had the pleasure' of being dragged around, through, and, yes, *under* a river by **Oncorhynchus tshawytscha** pulling like an unforgiving freight train at the other end of his line knows what I'm talking about when I state, categorically,

"I ain't never fly fishin' for kings again!"

Why would I say a thing like that in a book on fly fishing? Fly fishing for kings can definitely be classified as being a radical type of sport. Granted, there are times that it can *seem* fairly easy, but fly fishing for kings can also be frustrating, and it's *always* hard work.

Fly fishing for king salmon can do more to turn a fly fisherman into a rainbow trout fly fisherman than anything else I know of...

The first big king salmon I ever took on a long rod turned out to be a 45-pounder that dragged me around the river like a wet rag for about three hours before I was finally able to beach the thing. For a while there I thought the fish was going to win.

Then I started to get serious about the situation and made up my mind to end the battle for once and for all. I dug-in my heels and began cranking and pulling for all my worth. At the end I felt entirely exhausted and was gasping to catch my breath. Finally, an hour and a half later later, I reached down, subdued the fish, and nearly collapsed on the riverbank. I realized I had just finished a merciless battle with one of God's most wondrous creatures of the sea.

Earlier that morning, Greg Bell of *High Adventure Air Service* of Soldotna, Alaska had flown Clark Alvey and me in his deHavilland Beaver to the secluded king salmon river. We landed on a small, pristine lake and then made a short hike to the river. Unlike king salmon rivers that anglers can drive to, there were *no* other fishermen around us this day. Unbelievably, Clark and I had that world-class salmon river all to ourselves.

I couldn't believe the tenacity of that king...

Looking back, the only disappointment I felt from that trip was that I ended-up killing that big king. The way it had fought it had deserved better - at least a gentle release to freedom and to spawn. However, I hadn't lived in Alaska long at the time, and like many ignorant anglers, I was fairly unschooled about Alaska's fish species and sport fishing in general. I hadn't yet learned that the ultimate sport fishing victory comes only after subduing a quarry .....when releasing it, so the angler can feel the added excitement of seeing the fish swim away to freedom.

That's when the angler really feels the thrill of victory...

On another king salmon trip, a companion and I joined Doug and Danny Brewer of *Alaska West Air* flying out of Nikiski, or North Kenai.

That morning, along with another half-a-dozen anglers, we climbed aboard AWA's beautiful, red deHavilland Otter for a 30-minute flight across Cook Inlet to a small, tundra lake. Once there, my companion and I were transferred to AWA's Bell, 'Jet Ranger' Helicopter where we climbed-in and buck-

Alaska West Air's, Bell, 'Jet-Ranger II' Helicopter provides anglers the ultimate means of fishing Alaska's wild rivers.

led-up. Almost before we knew it, we were lifted-off to some of the most spectacular king salmon fishing either of us have ever experienced in our lives. *That* particular afternoon of fishing provided us with something like a dozen hook-ups apiece....something extremely extraordinary, to be sure. The kings were in 'so thick' it was almost like fishing for trout in a barrel. However, my elbow paid a stiff price for the festivities I enjoyed that day. Unless an angler has experienced it, it's difficult to imagine the amount of pain that nine or ten king salmon can cause on an elbow for the next few weeks following the fishing.

Frequently it's called, "Tennis Elbow," but those who know it as, "Fly-Fishing Elbow" know it hurts *just* the same.

Nevertheless, every once in a while I still find myself dreaming about that exciting afternoon of hooking umpteen fish in the twenty to forty pound class. Actually, just flying around in AWA's helicopter was about all the adventure any angler could ask for in the course of one day. Just being able to say to the pilot, ".. why don't we take 'er upstream another hole or two and take a peek around the corner..." qualified as being a surreal fishing experience.

As our helicopter pilot noted,"...*heli fishing is tough work, but somebody's got to do it...*"

Inexperienced salmon anglers need to understand that king salmon can really 'tear an angler up' on light tackle. Everybody wants to catch a king, but few anglers really understand what they're getting themselves into until they DO hook a fish that's about twenty-five times bigger than the largest trout they ever dreamed about...

It shouldn't surprise anybody that king salmon ruin more fishing reels in Alaska than does any other single sport fish specie. With a fish that can weigh up to sixty or seventy pounds, a fly fisher can get his money's worth in a hurry —*and then some.*

However, sometimes fishing for king salmon with a fly rod can turn out to be a very frustrating experience. The reason: often it's difficult just finding suitable water, or, simply finding water that isn't already infested with too many spoon-draggers and power boats. Sometimes when an angler *does* find water he can cast on with some degree of privacy, it's all but impossible to get the fly to

One of several 35-plus pound king salmon taken during fly-in with Alaska West Air *of North Kenai, Alaska.*

the fishing zone. Big, deep water, like that where kings are frequently found, can make it tough on a fly fisher. It's when you can see the shadows of where kings are stacked-up next to a beaver dam, but you can't get into a position to cast to them that can make for a particularly frustrating day of fishing. Sometimes an angler can find kings in secluded, very reachable spots, and these are the times he'll feel the enjoyment of king salmon fishing.

The heaviest king on record is a ***126 pounder*** that was taken commercially in the saltwater of Prince William Sound something approaching fifty years ago. Today you can see this very same mounted specimen on display at the Raspberry Office of the Alaska Department of Fish & Game in Anchorage. The current sport-fishing-caught record king salmon is a **97.4** pounder netted on 'gear' at the lower Kenai River in 1985. But kings these sizes are really the exception to the rule, however. Today's anglers would do well to expect to be dealing with fish in the 25 to 45-pound range. Not exactly new state records, but not exactly bluegills or crappies, either.

Most likely, what an angler will experience after hooking into his first king will be one of the most exhilarating chases he'll ever be involved in during his lifetime - especially if he manages to *survive* the experience. It's one thing for an angler to boast of catching a large king salmon using heavy spinning gear - and quite another to land one using a fly rod. That's the equivalent of a spin fisher using an Ultra-light for accomplishing a similar feat. One thing's for sure: those that do accomplish the task will never forget it.

King salmon go by many names: Kings are referred to as Chinook, Blackmouth, Tyee, and Spring Salmon. Some native groups call them by the name, 'Quinnat.'

The best times to fly fish for kings in Alaska are June and into mid- July, with the optimum time being somewhere in between, depending on the particular river you're fishing and that particular salmon run. But, kings can be found in Alaska's freshwater rivers and streams throughout the summer months in varying degrees of freshness, or 'condition.' Sometimes they can be found in what seem like the most outrageously small streams. There're even a couple of king salmon streams that flow through Anchorage.

Kings are found in the southern two thirds of the Alaska. Some of the best king salmon rivers that come to mind are: the Chuitna (Chuit), the Kenai, the Naknek, the Alagnak, the Goodnews, the Nushagak, the Togiak, the Karluk on Kodiak, and the Situk River near Yakutat. Of course, many other premier king fisheries can be found extending all the way from the picturesque saltwater regions of Prince of Wales Island near Ketchikan as far west as Kuskokwim Bay.

The excitement of the annual king salmon sport fishing in Alaska during June of each year is something to behold, a frenzy that probably accounts for at least one-third of Alaska's annual revenues - or so it seems during that time of year. Fishermen from all points of the globe flock to The Last Frontier in droves just to have a go at catching a king salmon - *some of them even attempting the feat using a fly rod.*

Alaska's king salmon anglers need to understand that kings are *not* the unlimited resource some individuals would have us believe they are. In reality, king salmon are a priceless commodity that must be protected and closely monitored. Alaska's anglers need to understand this and carefully release all king salmon hooked after filling a limit. Kings are simply too precious to waste.

The varying numbers of fish returning to the Kenai River annually are a good indication of how quickly king salmon stocks can fluctuate. Today, even though the numbers of returning fish appear to be on the increase, the Kenai fights to retain it's position as a premier king salmon fishery.

The Alaska record sport-caught king salmon weighed 97.4 pounds. It was caught on gear in 1985 by Alaskan Les Anderson at the lower Kenai River. As anyone who's fished Alaska can tell you, 97.4 pounds of king salmon is *some kind of trophy.* —🎣

Nanci Morris, head guide at 'Quinnat Landing Hotel' in King Salmon, Alaska with 50-pound, gear-caught king from Naknek River by her father, Wayne Braun.

How to Catch a King on a Fly

For those anglers out there who insist on giving kings 'a go' with a fly rod before they 'hang 'er up,' here's the king salmon prescription I recommend most. I believe this method, combined with a pinch of luck and a bit of patience, will, sooner or later, catch a fly fisherman a king salmon:

(1) Use a 10-weight fly rod, *minimum*.

(2) An 11-weight or12-weight rod would be better, yet.

(3) Use a high-density 20, or 24-foot sinking tip fly line like a Cortland Type 6, or a deep-water-express shooting head. The Teeny T-300 and T-400 fly lines are outstanding sink tips for fishing Alaska.

(4) Use OX (15 lb.) or stouter, 4-foot tapered leader tippet for kings.

(5) Look for "seams" where moderate currents meet swifter currents or where obstructions form 'holding water,' or deeper holes where incoming kings "stack up."

(6) Employ the services of size 2 , 1/0, or 2/0 weighted flies (a 'Fat Freddy' or a large Egg-Sucking Leech will do nicely) allowing the fly to get down and drift with the currents as it bounces deep, along the stream bottom into the mouths of resting salmon.

Fiberglass mounted 60-pound king salmon. Caution: kings this size can be hazardous to a flyrodder's health. Fish Mount by Ken Guffey.

(7 Make many, patient casts into likely-looking king water keeping as much slack out of your line as possible.

(8) When you feel you've caught a "snag" hold on tight and get ready for the fireworks. DON'T try to muscle the behemoth creature in during its first, powerful runs, whatever you do. Instead, use this time to 'set the hook' firmly by asserting a series of upward lifts, or jerks. (You'll probably want to use barbs while fishing for kings even though you may release them).

(9) Employ the drag on your reel or add additional braking by carefully palming your reel while playing fish - after they've begun to tire out a bit. Attempting to muscle a large king too early in a fight will often result in a lost fish or a broken reel, *or both*. All you're wanting to do a this stage of the fight is to tire the fish out. Usually, you'll find this takes some time, frequently an hour or more. When you finally get the fish beached you'll know you've really earned your trophy.

(10) Schedule an appointment with the elbow therapist and with the psychiatrist immediately after the fishing if you seriously intend to fly fish for kings anytime again in the near future.

SUPER SILVER
SALMON
Cohos

I t shouldn't surprise anyone much that **Oncorhynchus kisutch**, or the silver, coho, or *Silverside* salmon is the Alaska fly fisher's favorite of all five species of Pacific Salmon. This is because silvers are the most aggressive of all five species of Alaska's salmon...

Silver salmon are undoubtedly Alaska's premier calling cards during August of each year, especially to those flyrodders eager to hook into a fish that commonly goes airborne, commonly weighs between ten and thirteen pounds, and is well-known for it's aerial, tail-dancing, and cartwheeling displays.

Alaska's silvers are famed worldwide, and for good reason; *silver salmon strike flies with reckless abandon.* There's generally little or no hesitation involved - just *KaZam...*and they're there, flipping and cartwheeling at the end of your fly line, or feeling very much like you've hooked into a rainbow gone mad.

I personally don't take silver salmon fishing as seriously as I might (it occurs about the same time of year that many anglers also get serious about rainbows and steelhead) but I *do* take all of the silver salmon fly fishing I can get. Cohos on a fly rod make for great sport simply because it's fishing very similar to trophy rainbow fly fishing.

Now that it's officially recognized that rainbow trout and Pacific Salmon are more closely related than the biology books had us believing only a few years ago, it only makes sense why silvers cause the havoc they do when becoming hooked: Silvers are first cousins to rainbow trout. Flipping, cartwheeling, taildancing,....cohos walk away with the honors in the salmon aerial department - if not the pound for pound horsepower prize, itself. Some believe THAT honor should go to either the Chums or the Sockeyes.

In my travels across Alaska I've enjoyed many great days of fly fishing for silvers, but one of my most-memorable silver experiences came entirely by accident. Actually, I was Dolly Varden fishing at the time. As I fished my way around a bend of one of my favorite drive-to rivers, I stumbled upon a large school of resting silvers. All things considered, that afternoon was a very unusual set of circumstances, but then again, that's the way fly fishing can be at times.

Since Dollies were the only fish on my agenda that day, the only rod I had with me was an old, refinished Southbend bamboo dry fly rod, a short, seven-footer that had been rewrapped and refinished by Marty Karstetter, Alaska's master bamboo rod builder. However, I wasn't fishing dry flies; as I often do for Dolly fishing, I'd rigged the outfit with a weighted, pink, single-egg pattern, a floating line, and a long leader.

The sight of that school of silvers finning in those currents put an immediate change in my fishing plans, however...

If you can imagine standing waist-deep in a small, but gin-clear Alaskan stream, and quietly sneaking-up from behind, and then hooking ten and twelve-pound silvers on every fifth or sixth drift with a rod that feels like something of a toy, you'll know something of how I felt that clear, bright Saturday afternoon standing in the midst of those powerful salmon.

13-pound silver salmon taken by author at Alaska's Kamishak River. Note the size of the brown bear print in the foreground.

Whenever I'd hook one it would come flipping out of the water, showering me with spray, only to dash back in a hurry to 'the pack' for security, while I attempted to hold on for dear life. Eventually, each fish would finally tire-out a bit, and I'd carefully work it over to where I could tail it and remove the hook and release it. The action was fast and furious, and probably lasted about an hour and a half before the school started getting nervous and began moving upstream little by little. I remember wishing my Dad had been there with me that afternoon just so he'd know I wasn't exaggerating when I told him about it, later. It was silver salmon fly fishing at it's finest, available right off the main road, and there I was, just like Murphy's Law, with but a tiny bamboo trout rod, and hooking silvers like it was going out of style.

I could hear automobiles and trucks passing just a hundred or so yards away on the highway.

One of my best days, ever, for silver fishing occurred while fly fishing the Kamishak River, a few miles upstream of where it drains into Cook Inlet at Kamishak Bay. I was fishing with Bruce Johnson at the time, who's now managing Iliamna's *Red Quill Lodge.*

The Kami isn't very many miles away from famous McNeil River, so it goes without saying that brown bears are often present in the area. We must have seen a dozen brownies that day, but since the presence of bears often means fish are present, also, we viewed the bears as being a good omen.

I can only describe the silver salmon fishing we discovered that August day as being spectacular. What were the secrets for finding and catching them? We purposefully looked for slack-water offshoots where traveling salmon can "pull-over" and make a rest stop. When you've located one of these areas, try casting a size-2 Flash Fly or large, Egg-Sucking Leech on a Teeny, T-300 or T-200 line, let it sink a bit, and then begin stripping—and hold on and get ready for action. Even when encountered resting from their upstream journies, silvers are powerful fighters. We must have each hooked and released a couple of dozen silvers that afternoon by the way my arm ached later that evening.

But, that's often the way it is with silvers—frequently it's an all or nothing affair. They're either in —*and hitting* —or they're not. It can be as simple as that.

One of the latest crazes I've heard about recently is, 'float tubing for silvers.' I haven't tried it, yet, but two of my good friends, Tom Coomer and Tee Blair, both of Anchorage, apparently make several pilgrimages to Kodiak Island each fall just to experience float tubing for powerhouse silver

Author with a mint-bright silver salmon hooked by stripping silver and orange 'Flash Fly' through temporary resting water using an 8-weight fly rod.

salmon. They both swear it's 'float tubing at it's finest,', that it makes for a great getaway weekend, and that the only 'fly in the ointment' might be the distances they sometimes have to kick themselves back after being pulled around by a fish of seemingly several horsepower. Like I say, I haven't tried it yet, but I *hope to* one of these days. It sounds like the perfect way to try-out my new float tube.

The best months for fly fishing for Silver Salmon are August and September, with some larger fish returning to freshwater as late as **October and**

November.

Alaska's silver salmon anglers will want to check with local guides about the best times for individual runs and where to find fish. My good friend, Tim Hiner, (no relation) a pro fishing guide on the Kenai, probably knows as much about Alaska's silver salmon as anyone. Tim has operated out of Soldotna, Alaska for a dozen years, or more.

Like the kings, **Silver salmon are found in the Southern two thirds of Alaska.** Saltwater estuaries are often prime spots for locating silvers. Look for slack water resting areas along riversides (I call them Cul-de-sacs) where schools of cohos will pull over to rest and mill about during their upstream migrations. Also look for "seams" where faster water converges with moderate water - because silver salmon (like steelhead) like to lie-up in these spots and rest before continuing upstream.

Alaskan photographer and guide, Eberhard Brunner, captured this close-up of 'coho' or silver salmon.

Watch for silvers stacking-up at riffles, too, for riffles are great aerating zones, where tired salmon will lie-up, take-in oxygen, and refresh themselves for continuing their journey. Riffles are good places to find fish holding. Fish seem to sense they are somewhat protected in riffles by the water's broken surface.

Anglers can easily pick-out these places if they'll stop and examine a river's varying currents for a minute or two. Cast the fly quartering upstream past the spot where the confluence begins - then allow it to sink and tumble through the suspected "bucket" or "holding zone." Have faith in yourself and in your instincts and allow the fly to drift in a natural method past the suspected "hot spot." Chances are good that your sixth sense will point out areas where silvers are to be found.

Flash Flies, Egg-Sucking Leeches, and large Fall Favorites have been as effective as any patterns I've ever used on silvers - with black & brown Woolly Buggers performing admirably, also. 1X (tapered to a 12 lb. tippet) is usually about the correct ticket for leader tippet strength for fly fishing for cohos, and a stout 8-weight or 9-weight rod is about right for the task of handling silvers. Over the years I've relied on a fast actioned, 9-foot, 9-weight Orvis Boron/Graphite fly rod with excellent results. I got the rod as extra gravy in a rod deal with John Scott back in Connecticut a few years ago, and it's proved to be a very lucky fly rod for me.

As in most salmon fishing, employ a high-density sink tip line to get down quickly in moving water, or try stripping a flashy, size-2 fly through likely-looking holding, or resting water.

Then watch out! Silvers strike voraciously. Before you know it, the battle will be raging.

Some of the great silver streams that come to mind are: the Kenai, the Togiak, the Alagnak, the Goodnews, ...the list goes on and on.

For those anglers who've yet to experience fly fishing for **kisutch,** be advised that the sport can become addictive. And, yes, under the right conditions silvers *can* be taken at the surface, a sport that those who've experienced rave about. I've yet to try it, but many anglers swear that deer hair mouse patterns and large muddlers on the surface perform admirably, indeed.

One of the keys to great silver salmon fishing is finding them just out of

Tom Coomer float Tubing for silvers

saltwater in 'intertidal zones,' or just upstream as they've entered freshwater to travel to begin spawning. A number of rivers come to mind whenever I think of great silver fishing I've enjoyed, but most of 'em have been near the saltwater, except the Kenai, just where it drains out of Skilak Lake.

Whenever possible, practice catch and release on Alaska's salmon. Regardless of what some anglers may try to tell you, silvers are not a never-ending commodity. Consider taking just enough for the freezer and allowing any extras to go to complete their spawning chores. Silvers make for fine dining, even though most anglers consider either red salmon or kings to be superior in taste to silvers.

The Alaska record Silver Salmon was a 26 pounder taken in 1976. *Just thinking about hooking into a fish that size on a fly rod gives me a case of the shakes...*

CHUMS, CALICOS, OR SILVERBRITE SALMON

laska's honors for the most underrated fish have to go to the chum salmon, or **Oncorhynchus keta** - for those who might tend to prefer the official, or scientific name. I'm certainly no authority on **keta,** but I do know this: Chums can rip a spool free of backing as fast as any fish in Alaska. Hook into a bright chum just a few hundred yards above saltwater and you'll learn, very quickly, what I'm talking about. And, on occasion, chums will even supply anglers with some exciting top water action in the form of half-gainers and backflips.

Besides their reserves of power, chum salmon also own the distinction of having more names than any other fish in Alaska. Some people call them Chums, some call them Calicos (denoting their variegated, vertical stripes found along their sides) and some still refer to them as, 'Dog Salmon,' or simply, '*Dogs,*' a term derived from Alaska's natives feeding them to their dog teams during Alaska's long, cold winters.

But the name I like most for chums is: *Silverbrites.* It's a name that really seems to fit - especially when an angler is standing waist-deep in a large, roily Alaskan river with schools of hundreds of these powerful, bright fish finning past in all directions. If you've never had the pleasure of snapping a brand new, shiny, expensive, state-of-the-art fly rod on your very first cast, you simply haven't lived, and chum salmon can cause this to happen as quickly as any fish in the north. I've experienced this very thing, so I know for a certainty: a fresh chum being the culprit.

Chums have what I call 'raw horsepower,' especially when they're mint-bright, just in from the salt. They can really pour on the power, and the best example I can give to mirror this is to tell about the time I made my first cast with an expensive, new 9-weight rod, hooking a fresh chum in the process. As the fish bolted to escape, the shiny graphite rod snapped like a pretzel, sounding somewhat like a .300 Winchester Magnum exploding in my ear as it did so. Somehow I managed to finally 'tail' and release that fish, but don't ask me how, or to repeat the process again. I had to borrow my guide's personal 10-weight rod for the remainder of the trip.

Chum salmon average between 7 to 11 pounds, occasionally going to 15 or 18 pounds. **The Alaska record chum, taken in 1985, went a full 32 pounds.**

Bobby DeVito, owner of *Branch River Lodge* on the Alagnak, introduced me to one of my favorite chum flies, a size-2 pink and purple creation called a,

'Popsicle.' Bobby explained it was a fly he'd first learned about from his father, Dr. Bob DeVito, Sr., and I must admit, it's been my experience that chums strike these flies like piranhas do cattle, regardless of what some anglers will say about chums having a case of "lockjaw" at times. A purple Egg-Sucking Leech will usually accomplish the same results nicely, also, and I've had good results on chum salmon when using a silvery, "Flash Fly," too. In currents, chums seem particularly attracted to tumbling flash.

Bobby DeVito, Jr., owner of Branch River Lodge, *with nice, fresh chum on Alagnak (or Branch River) just a couple of miles upstream from confluence with Kvichak.*

One of the secrets of fishing for chums (as well as all species of Alaska's Pacific Salmon) is getting down *deep* to where the fish are to be found. Some anglers waste countless hours drifting or stripping flies over the heads of salmon when, in reality, all they'd need to do is employ the services of a high-density sinking-tip line and a short, 4-foot leader. Strip a silvery 'Flash Fly,' a big, ugly Egg-Sucking Leech, or a pink and purple 'Popsickle' through a school of resting or milling *silverbrites,* and get ready for action.

There's a good chance the majority of Alaska's visitors will be surprised when a silverbrite salmon decides to move to the next county. Pound for pound, 'ol calico might just walk away with the honors in the All-Alaskan power to weight department. They're more than a little surprising on a fly rod, trust me.

Suggested fly rods for chum salmon: 9-weight or 10-weight. These might sound like a lot of rod, but they're about right, and in fact, I'd take the 10-weight hands down over the 9-weight as a 'chum salmon' rod.

Suggested methods for hooking chums: look for congregating, milling schools. Then cast over them, and strip through suspected holding areas. In swift-moving water, try tumbling a silvery, 'Flash Fly' along the bottom to holding fish. Chums are highly attracted to bright, flashy patterns. Use a high-density sink tip line to get the fly down quickly to where the salmon are holding or milling about.

Best months for Oncorhynchus keta are, July and August, and a few days into September. Employ stout 1X (or 12 lb. mono) or OX leaders to hold chums, and having a reel with a fairly decent drag system will prove to be appreciated, too. Chum salmon are found throughout the entire state - with the exception of a few found just along the Canadian border, south of Eagle.

Chum salmon flesh is okay if dried or smoked, but it is *not* generally considered as being among the best tasting of the five species of Alaska's Pacific Salmon.

And, just in case you're wondering, there's no better fish in Alaska than 'ol Calico to prepare an angler for king salmon on a fly...

Author with 14-pound chum caught on 10-weight fly rod using pink and purple, 'Popsicle" streamer stripped deep, through holding water using Teeny, T-300 sink tip fly line.

SOCKEYE (RED) SALMON

Bluebacks

O ne of my very favorite sport fish is a strange trophy in the sense that it's officially a plankton eater and therefore has no business whatsoever striking at flies. However, sockeyes don't always strike at flies, but rather, 'nip' at them. That's when all the fun begins.

Pound for pound, at least in my book, anyway, along with the chums, sockeye salmon just might be *the* strongest fighters of all five species of Pacific Salmon.

Nobody ever comes out and actually states that, however, probably because sockeyes are so common that it only seems right that Alaska's toughest fighters should be an exotic, hard to locate fish...

'Blueback,' or fresh sockeye (or red) salmon. Pound for pound, considered by many to be one of Alaska's scrappiest sport fish. Bluebacks are very tenacious and can sometimes be difficult to hook on a fly rod. Fish mount by Ken Guffey, The Fish Specialist.

One particular bend of the Kenai River down near the Great Alaska Fish Camp evokes very fond sockeye salmon fly fishing

memories for me. Why? It was there that I caught my very first sockeye on a flyrod years ago, a spectacular, fresh, strong 'blueback,' a sockeye salmon just in from the salt. GAFC Manager Lawrence John and guide Mike Murri had no sooner pointed to where I might cast my 9-weight sink-tip...when...WHAM! A blueback hit and turned in fast currents. Before I knew it that fish had about seventy-five yards of backing out and was still in the process of moving downstream at an alarming pace.

Before that day I wasn't aware that a salmon that's not a king could provide power like that.

'Bluebacks' have a way of testing even the most experienced angler's skills — especially when they're hooked in fast water, like those found at the confluence of intersecting rivers. When hooked, sockeyes often peel off, and head directly for faster water, allowing the currents to greatly aid them in their getaway. Sockeyes' fights are tenacious, and each year, tens of thousands of residents and visitors, alike, flock to Alaska's sockeye (red salmon) rivers, just to have a go at the thrill of hooking into these powerful, tasty fighters.

Skyrocketing sockeyes, they're called...

It doesn't hurt matters much, either, that red salmon are considered by most people to be among the very best tasting of Alaska's five species of Pacific salmon.

After red's have been in fresh water for a few days, they begin a drastic color change; suddenly their bodies become a deep, red color, while their heads become what I've best heard described as a 'parrot' green.

Mark Thunell with a large red salmon in spawning phase. Ironically, Mark landed and released this huge sockeye using a 4-weight fly rod. He had been fishing for Dolly Varden char at the time.

At this time of spawning sockeyes become a much easier fish to hook then when they've just arrived from the salt. After they've 'turned,' and begin fertilizing eggs in redds (or nests) sockeyes begin to snap at any likely object or fly pattern that looks as if it might be invading their temporary spawning domain. However, before sockeyes 'turn color,' they can be a real challenge to hook and bring to hand on a fly.

'Two of my favorite places for fishing for fresh, incomming bluebacks are the Kenai River, at the confluence of the Moose and the Kenai near *Great Alaska Fish Camp* at Sterling, Alaska - and at the remarkable Newhalen River, just below the falls, about a half mile upstream from where the river spills into Lake Iliamna. There are others, of course, one of the most famous red salmon fisheries being the popular Russian River just where it enters the Kenai.

The Kvichak River, (the outlet of Iliamna) is superb sockeye country, proclaimed to be among the finest in the world. Ask 'Big John' Hutchinson at *Big Mountain Lodge* on the Kvichak about fly fishing for sockeye salmon. 'Big John' has probably landed and released as many sockeyes over the past fifteen years as anyone in the state.

Typical weights for **Oncorhynchus nerka** go from 6 to 9 pounds, with some larger subspecies going to ten, or even eleven pounds.

July 4th usually marks the beginning of red salmon fishing each summer throughout Alaska, and **July is definitely the best month for red salmon, or sockeye fishing throughout Alaska.**

Although it's popular to suggest 7-weight fly rod outfits for sockeyes, Alaska's best

Bob Singer with a typical, Brooks River sockeye salmon taken during 1st week of July.

sockeye salmon rods are actually the 8-weight or 9-weight outfits. I still find myself relying on an old, battle-scarred Orvis Boron/Graphite 9-weight that has proven to be very lucky for me over the years. I prefer the Teeny sink-tip series of lines for sockeye fishing, with the T-200 or T-300 lines being my personal favorites.

First timers might want to be sure they rely on reels featuring modern drag systems, but fly fishing for sockeyes with 'conventional,' non-drag 'trout reels' can make for superb fishing fun. It boils down to the amount of time an angler wants to devote to playing a fish. If he can enjoy the battle for a while, conventional reels are 'entirely adequate.'

One thing's for certain: fresh sockeyes will earn an angler's respect on a fly rod, assuming the angler can master the technique of hooking reds in the first place.

If only sockeyes would attack a fly with a little more ferocity...

Nevertheless, red salmon are considered by many to be the best tasting of

Alaska *on the Fly*

Alaska's five species of pacific salmon, unless you happen to be of the other persuasion (as I am) who believe that kings rank as number one in the taste department.

The Alaska record sockeye (or red) salmon, taken from the Kenai River in 1974 weighed 16 pounds, 0 oz. Hook into a blueback like that ...especially in fast currents...

.... and you'll have your hands full, believe me!

The author with a large 'blueback,' or fresh sockeye (red) salmon taken on Iliamna's Newhalen River. He was fishing a Teeny T-300 sink tip line on a 9-weight at the time. Photo by John Gierach.

Bluebacks' are really the only sockeyes worth bragging about. Here are some of the secrets I've learned about successfully landing them with a fly rod:

(1) Best success in hooking Bluebacks often comes in moderate to swift-moving waters. When an angler comes upon a school of sockeyes milling about in a slow-water resting spot, often they're too easily snagged, or 'foul-hooked' on fins or flanks, and there is no real sport to be found. To get sockeyes to ' take' a fly, look for swifter water, such as riffles or a conflu-ence, where a main river and a secondary tributary meet. This is where you're likely to find resting salmon, right along the bottom, where they'll be lying-up regaining their strength.

(2) Use a high-density sink-tip line if the water you are fishing has any depth to it at all. In shallower waters, an angler can get away with fishing a floating line and employing split shot above the fly to help get down. Remember - getting down to pacific salmon in fresh water is extremely important. Other wise, the angler can spend wasted hours drifting flies over hundreds of salmon all day long without success.

(3) Employ the services of a sparsely-tied size-2 brown, purple, or black streamer. (Mike Hershberger relied on a dark creation he hailed a winner he named, *'Fred The Red'* which looked very much like a dark pheasant tail, or Teeny Nymph). Now, cast upstream, and quartering across the currents, allowing the fly to sink and begin drifting with the current in the direction of the salmon. Bounce the fly along the river's bottom into a 'seam' full of waiting salmon, directly into their opening and closing jaws - maximizing your chances of enticing a sockeye to snap at your fly.

(4) Keep a minimum of slack in your line, and

(5) Hold on for dear life after you feel the 'take.' Chances are, first timers will be surprised at the power of sockeye salmon.

PINK SALMON
Beginner's Dream Fish

I f someone were to ask me, "..what's the one, best specie for kids learning to fly fish?" I'd have no choice but to answer, "Pink salmon (or Humpies) of course, *No* question about it!" Pinks definitely aren't the prettiest fish an angler will ever lay his eyes on, in fact, a male "Humpy" can look downright disgusting at times with it's long, gholish snout and it's outlandish, sharply humped back. Tee-shirts depicting Alaska's pink salmon entitled, "Humpies From Hell," are commonly seen being worn around Alaska.

But Pink Salmon have the wonderful attribute of gobbling flies of every assorted shape and color thrown at them, and because of this they are a great fish to learn on with a fly rod- for a time, at least, until the fly fisher gets bored or wears down from a case of sore wrists.

I call Resurrection Creek, located at the town of Hope, Alaska (across Turnagain Arm of Cook Inlet from Anchorage) the

"Humpy," or male Pink salmon. Pinks might not be Alaska's most sought-after fish, but they are a 'perfect' fish for beginning fly fishers. This pink was captured by Bret Huber, the photo was taken by Evan Swensen

'pink salmon capitol of the world.' Actually, there are tens of other rivers in Alaska with as many pinks, it's just that Resurrection Creek is accessible to the average Alaskan with an automobile and enough gasoline for an hour's drive...a great place for a beginner to learn to fly fish.

Oncorhynchus gorbuscha, *or* Pacific Pink Salmon, are the smallest of Alaska's five salmon species. But they're also among the most prolific, and **especially in ODD years** when they arrive at Alaska's intertidal areas in the hundreds of thousands to spawn. All of a sudden, they're just there..."Pinks by the Zillions!" If you look into the water of many streams you can see their "white and black' appearances as they lie there, finning in the currents.

Although a "Hen Humpy" can be a fairly normal-looking fish (sometimes even resembling a trout at first glance) it's those "Humpies From Hell," the bucks, or males, that are often ugly enough to frighten off an entire regiment of Royal Canadian Mounties.

Pinks average 3 to 5 pounds, but some of the old males will far outweigh that mark, easily going 7 or 8 pounds. The **Alaska record Pink salmon weighed 12 pounds 9 ounces.** It was taken near *The Great Alaska Fish Camp* where the Moose River enters the Kenai.

Pinks are often fished for using 6-weight and 7-weight fly rods.

The best times to fish for pinks are mid-July and into

This pink salmon was quickly photographed and released. Having a small pocket camera handy will add greatly to the fly fisher's overall experience.

August, with ODD years being far superior for numbers of fish.

Pinks are found at most intertidal areas surrounding Alaska, from saltwater inland approximately 20 miles. If you're looking for pink salmon in numbers, fish near the salt.

Humpies are not known for remaining prime, or 'fresh' for any length of time once they've entered fresh water to begin their spawning.

Yet, whatever their minuses, pinks have one thing in their favor over all other salmon species found in Alaska: Never was there a fish better designed for kids or for beginners on a fly rod than a fresh-from-the-salt, *if ugly,* pink salmon.

...and the good news is, they'll strike at almost any fly you throw at 'em...

The Sport of Fly Fishing
Provides Man With A Way To
Nourish His Soul and Find
Breathing Room For His Spirit
...Whether He Catches Any Fish, or Not.
-Anonymous

The road that you wander is the road
that you choose. The day that you tarry
is the day that you lose... J. Johnson

DOLLY VARDEN & ARCTIC CHAR

I n my opinion, the poor, badly-maligned Dolly Varden char, or 'Goldenfin' is actually one of the noblest fishes to swim Alaska's waters. I say this defiantly and somewhat blatantly for good reason: I firmly believe the Dolly Varden char deserves to be considered as one of Alaska's *most respected* sport fish —instead of being considered just a common fish of sorts, a fish accused of consuming too many salmon eggs - and thus being 'harmful to salmon survival.'

Commercial fishermen dislike 'em because they blame the Dollies and char for 'hogging the industry...'

Everybody swears it's the arctic char, or **Salvelinus alpinus**, that's the hero of the two, but it 's the Dolly Varden that's the most numerous of the two

Dolly Varden char before release. Dollies and char don't jump like rainbows, but fight deep with twisting motions. Char often signal a reflective 'Flash' when they turn to intercept a fly.

species and is officially considered to be an **anadromous** fish, while there are those who swear up and down the arctic char is a freshwater-only specie. However, there are others who'll assure you it, too, is anadromous.

Actually, research has shown that both arguments are correct: In fact, if you really want to get technical about it, *four* subspecies technically exist, a char and a Dolly that ARE anadromous, and a char and a Dolly that exist entirely in freshwater. Let's see, that makes one, two, three....four ...subspecies of char.

There's always been the on-going discussion about the difference between

the two species - and I've even talked with Fish & Game Biologists on different occasions who've been in total disagreement with each other regarding some of the traits of Dollies and arctic char.

It *wouldn't seem right if there weren't opposing opinions...would it?*

Then, there's the issue about the difference between the spots of the two. "The arctic char has pink and orange spots on its sides *larger* than the pupils of its eyes," *experts purport*, while the Dolly Varden wears pink and orange spots 'smaller than it's pupils." One can

Chunky, 4-pound char taken while 'nymphing' a single-egg pattern. By using a long leader and a floating line, fly fishers can obtain 'natural' drifts. Photo by Mark Thunell.

also attempt to distinguish between the two species by counting their gill rakers, or, by cutting into the fish's stomach and counting the *pyloric caeca* muscles, and then make a determination.

But, who wouldn't rather be fishing than counting gill rakers or performing stomach surgery?

Like many fly fishermen who fly fish Alaska frequently, I've enjoyed many delightful hours of catching and releasing Dolly

John Gierach 'nymphing' for char in Alaska's Iliamna river country. Often, if an angler looks closely, he'll start to 'see' the indistinct silhouettes of char lying near the bottoms of many of Alaska's premier rivers.

Varden 'trout' on a fly rod. As any dyed-in-the-wool fly fisherman can tell you, it's difficult for a fellow to get that intimate with *any* fish for long and not begin to appreciate it ....just a little, anyway...

It's not that arctic char aren't entirely beautiful, mind you. They're a *gorgeous* fish. But a Dolly Varden char is nearly as colorful as its brother, the arctic char, and it's the Dolly that occupies the entirety of Alaska's regions, while the arctic char is to be found only in the extreme northwest part of the state, from

Bristol Bay south down into the Alaska Peninsula, and on Kodiak and Afognak Islands. Try locating a true, arctic char in many places in Alaska's interior and you'll be looking for a good, long time.

Dollies and char aren't jumpers like rainbows, but they are good, stout fighters nonetheless. They tend to 'fight deep,' twisting and turning

This beautiful arctic char from Alaska's Wood River /Tikchik Lakes region came to an Olive Woolly Bugger stripped in a fast retrieve near the surface. John Gierach photo.

when hooked, and it's one of their traits that as they approach a fly to take it, they'll signal a flash to the surface to 'tip off' the fisherman that it's time to 'set the hook' or tighten the line. When the angler sees this happen, or the end of his

fly line twitches (or his strike indicator wiggles) it's time to lift the rod and begin the battle.

Another pleasing characteristic about the char family (including lake trout) are their strikingly-beautiful, white-striped fins. These bright-white fin markings appear to be almost surreal at times and always astound me, particularly when char are also wear-

Plump Kenai Peninsula Dolly Varden char was caught , photographed, and released, all within a matter of seconds.

ing their full-color bronze and deep-green spawning colors to go with their white, pin-striped fins.

As for fodder for char, "Iliamna Pinkies," those tiny, pink, chenille-tied single salmon egg imitations, are ultra-effective in the taking of char, Dollies, or lake trout. Those slightly larger single egg patterns, called 'Glo-Bugs,' are also exceptional producers, as are two-egg patterns such as the famed 'Babine Special' and 'Two Egg Sperm Fly.' Of course, the old, reliable 'Polar Shrimp' takes it's share of char, also.

Alaska *on the Fly*

There are some traditionalists who continually argue that 'naturals' like gold-ribbed hares ear nymphs, etc., should be the patterns of choice for taking Dollies nobly, but my reply has always been, "Why try to please some purist's tastes when Alaska's Dollies and char are keying-in on salmon eggs?

Mike Hershberer tried to nail me on this point once at Brooks a few years ago but my reply seemed to steal the wind from his sails:

"If Egg-Patterns are so unethical, I asked him, why is it that *You* stock and sell Egg-Sucking Leeches in your fly shop, Mike?" Hershberger was a man with a quick, dry wit, but this was one time he didn't seem to have a quick reply. Maybe most fishermen *aren't* Einsteins, but we ain't necessarily stupid, either. Employing the charms of a single-egg pattern is simply Alaska's version of 'matching the hatch.'

Do you want to catch fish or do you just want to spend time going through the motions?

During Alaska's salmon season, what could make more sense than fishing a small, single-egg pattern? To refute that logic would

A trophy, 7-pound arctic char taken in Alaska's Ugashik Lakes region. Photo by Dr. Leon 'Joe' Chandler, of King Salmon's Quinnat Landing.

be akin to refusing to fish a "Flesh Fly" in the fall only because imitating decaying salmon flesh doesn't qualify as being a 'classy,' traditional way of fly fishing. What about Bonefishers? Should they continue throwing Crab imitations or should they all become traditionalists and resort to throwing Pale Morning Duns?

But, there are times when Fry and Smolt patterns are the ticket; when fishing early in the season, late in the season, or while fishing lakes, try tumbling or stripping "a smolt pattern" and expect good results.

Char fishing is frequently best when the angler understands they are usually found lying deep, finning at or near stream bottoms. Often char appear as 'Grey Ghosts' as they lie at stream bottoms, nearly imperceptibly as they do. Often, it takes a bit of a 'trained eye' to be able to pick out char consistently.

Fly fishing for char is often best accomplished when utilizing the pleasures of a floating line, a long leader, and by crimping-on a split shot or two approximately 18" up from an egg-pattern. This way the angler can watch the end of his fly line as it floats, while the egg-pattern bobs along in a natural manner, to the char lying in wait specifically to intercept these loose, drifting eggs. Call it nymphing, call it bouncin' eggs, call it what ever you like... *but it sure is fun.*

Whereverfly fishermen encounter either of these two char species there will be much entertainment to be enjoyed....whether the fisherman calls 'em Dollies ...or arctic char.

Alaska's Dollies, arctic char, and lake 'trout' all sport stylish, white-striped fins. All are members of the 'char' family and share similar, distinguishing characteristics, including 'forked tail.'

One way a fisherman can make sure he doesn't offend any of his listeners is, refer to both Dollies and arctic char as.....*char.*

It is purported by some that arctic char tend to average a bit more in weight than Dolly Varden, but this can only be because arctic char are often found in more remote, inaccessible, and unfished areas. Dolly Varden char average 2 to 5 pounds. **The Alaska record was a 17 pound 8 ounce char** taken up north from the Wulik River where it flows into the sea near Kotzebue. **The best months for fishing for arctic char are June, and then again in September and October,** although some systems reach their peaks for char as early as July.

Dollies are found in greatest numbers during July, August, and September, depending upon the length of the salmon runs and the numbers of loose, drifting salmon eggs present at that particular time.

So, you can call 'em Dollies, or you can call 'em arctic char, it's entirely up to you. Hopefully you'll be correct at least half of the time, anyway.

Me? I'm not taking any chances. From now on, I'm simply calling both species.... "*char.*"

LAKE TROUT

L ake trout, a.k.a.'Mackinaw,' a.k.a. 'Lakers,' a.k.a. **Salvelinus namaycush** (or dweller of the deep) are, to my eyes at least, one of the most beautiful fishes of the north country—and especially during the fall when they're wearing their spawning colors.

If you can imagine a dorsal and back of lobster shell green, variegated with vermiculated splotches of pale blue extending down onto blue-green sides with tiny colored spots of silver, gold, yellow and blues, with a rusty-white belly and with striking, burnt-orange tinted fins capped off by brilliant white stripes at the leading edges... you'll have *some* idea of what a colorful fellow a lake trout really is. Yet, despite all this color the lake trout's deeply forked tail is considered it's most distinguishing characteristic.

The lake trout's eyes are large, dark and clear in contrast to their beautifully colored bodies. A member of the char family, lake trout are not officially 'trout' at all, but are in fact, a bonafide member of the char family. Like char, lake trout usually 'sound deep' and twist a lot after becoming hooked. Unlike rainbows, however, lake trout don't spend much time going airborne.

There seems to be a certain mystique about fly fishing for lake trout. Often, lakers are found at Alaska's most isolated, wilderness lakes and streams, where they prefer icy, clear waters. Often there is a pristine, wilderness setting inherent with the best lake trout waters. Picture a lonely loon calling from a clear, high-mountain lake and you're starting to get the picture.

Lake trout make for an enchanting, challenging specie on a fly rod.

I'll never forget the first time I took a laker on a fly. The fish was a single, solitary deep 'cruiser' who's shadow had been spotted by a member of our party as it roved the waters of a brilliantly clear, exceedingly pristine backcountry lake. It was approximately high-noon when the laker was first noticed, one of the last times I'd ever expect to find myself sight fishing to a lake trout.

Actually, I wasn't even fishing at the time, but was busy enjoying a sandwich after experiencing an exceptional morning of fly fishing for arctic grayling. For lunch, our pilot had taxied us over in the floatplane to a lovely, secluded beach where we could enjoy the view as we propped ourselves up against a log near the beach. The lake we were at was surrounded by beautiful, snow-capped mountains which reflected from the water's surface in perfect symmetry.

The way I saw it, there was nothing for me to do but have a go at it.

I'd been using a pet, 9-foot 5-weight Sage fly rod that morning for grayling, one of a handful of beautiful graphite rods that Dave Angus at Mountain View Sports in Anchorage has put together for me.

Realizing I'd probably have to 'go down deep after that fish' I unclipped my Griffith's Gnat dry fly and reached for a weighted 'Iliamna Pinkie,' (a single-egg pattern closely resembling a salmon egg) that I figured might serve to attract the laker's attention as it sunk. Quickly, I also added a split-shot about 18 inches up the leader from the fly, knowing I'd have to get the fly down to have any real chance for that fish.

After wading out to where I stood almost chest deep in the clear lake, and spotting the fish's cruising shadow on the lake's bottom, I worked out a long length of fly line in a series of false casts and made my delivery. As luck would have it, and as though it were something I did every day of my life, I 'led' the target a bit so as to give the fly time to sink and intercept the fish.

Suddenly the laker was there!

I'd actually hooked it! Lifting the rod, I set the hook to the knob of the pinched barb.

After a decent but not especially powerful battle, the beautiful little six or seven pound lake trout came to hand. I was more than a bit impressed with it's beautiful colorations. I had been careful not to rush the fishing experience by 'horsing' the fish.

During the fight the laker had tried to bore down, or 'sound.' Like I said, it's resistance to the rod was solid, but not fervent. It's orange and white fins and beautiful, vermiculated blue and green back were astoundingly colorful against it's rusty white belly. It's eyes were dark and very clear, seeming to be very large for a fish its' size.

I knew I had been very lucky to take that lake trout as things happened. Fortunately the laker had turned in the direction of the egg-pattern and somehow the fly had dropped the ten or twelve feet necessary for interception.

I became hooked on lake trout fishing that day. My friend bet me that I couldn't catch it and I've since taken him up on lunch.

Since that day I've enjoyed other opportunities for lake trout, although, strangely, for some reason or other, I've never made a fishing trip specifically with lake trout in mind. As they are for most anglers, lake trout have always been a secondary specie opportunity for me.

If I had to take a lake trout to save my life, it wouldn't be with a dry fly on a lonely lake, nor would it be with a deeply-sunken fly at a lake, either. Instead, I would opt to fish the inlets or outlets of some of Iliamna's larger lakes, just where the currents converge and begin to flow quickly. Kukaklek and Naknek

Lakes are prime examples. Places like these are where lakers spend a good deal of their time, hovering in the moderate currents, ready to intercept food as it passes. After all, lake trout don't grow to be giants by not eating.

The remote waters of Skilak Lake might be as good a place as any for a fly rodder from the city to catch himself his first laker. Try a calm summer's evening, around nine or ten o'clock, after it's cooled down a bit. Then, pick-out a lonely, secluded bay or cove, and decide whether you'll opt to fish with a dry fly on the surface or strip a "smolt pattern."

When anglers start getting into waters the caliber of Lake Louise they'll start getting into real lake trout fishing. In the early spring, or in the fall, Kukaklek, where it empties into *The Branch* is to be considered as one of the state's premier lake trout spots.

Lake trout are really members of the char family and not a trout at all. During summer months lake trout will be found in deep, cold water, throughout most of Alaska. They may be readily caught in shallow water right after break-up and just before freeze-up. The State record is 47 pounds. Minimum state of Alaska trophy award weight is 20 pounds.

The best times to fly fish for Alaska's lake trout are: June, and then again when it begins to cool down a bit in **September and October.** Often, especially in the spring, lakers can be taken on streamers imitating small fish, like 'Black Nose Dace,' or a 'Gray Ghost' or the like. Also, try the various 'smolt' patterns. During spawning, mature males will scurry smolts and smaller fish away from their redds (or nests), so employing a streamer is often an effective strategy. Lake trout fishing often means cautious, careful fishing. You won't want to disturb the natural setting much. On lakes, where an angler finds lakers on the rise or feeding at or near the surface, he's found a wonderful opportunity for great fishing. Whether fishing from a boat, from a float tube, or from a concealed lakeshore position, cautiously work a line out to the appropriate distance and make a delicate presentation using a tiny artificial dry fly. If you're fishing a wet fly or a streamer or a leech pattern and using a sinking line, or even a high-density sink-tip, allow it to sink for a few seconds (count to varying 'thousands' to find the correct depth) and then begin stripping the fly back to you - employing varying lengths of pull, and by adding erratic, lifelike movements to the fly. When you feel like you've suddenly caught a 'snag,' you'll be surprised to learn you've hooked a lake trout instead.

Leeches, Sculpins, Zonkers, or Minnow imitations are good choices on lakers, also. And, yes, lake trout can be taken on dry flies, especially during summer at lake outlets or in moderately shallow streams where concentrated food sources funnel, or from the surface of lakes and streams when other food items are scarce. Mosquitos, Gnats, Wullfs, Parachutes, Adams'...all will take lakers on occasion.

Lake trout are distributed in two major areas of Alaska: In the north they can be found in a band reaching from the Beaufort Sea extending southwest to the Kobuk River. In the south of Alaska lake trout are found along the southern third of the state west into the Alaska Peninsula. Some western regions of the Alaska' panhandle' also hold lesser amounts of lake trout.

Equipment for lakers? If I were going after lake trout specifically, I'd be tempted to use an 8-weight fly rod for it's distance and wind-bucking capabilities. I'd want the rod to be at least 9 feet long, and fishing a ten-footer would provide great fun. A little heavier rod allows an angler to throw larger, weighted flies when needed, but dry flies can still be enjoyed, too.

The Alaska record for lake trout is a fish that weighed 47 pounds, 0 oz. caught at Clarence Lake in 1970. But *you'll* have a good time anytime you can hook into lakers weighing forty pounds less than the record fish, believe me, even though officially, they're lake *char*...

...*not* lake *trout.*

If its solitude you're seeking have an air taxi service fly you to a high mountain Alaska lake and fish for rainbows and grayling with a dry fly. Photo by Joe Caterinichio, DDS.

ARCTIC GRAYLING

ARISTOCRATS OF THE NORTH

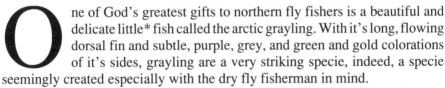

O ne of God's greatest gifts to northern fly fishers is a beautiful and delicate little* fish called the arctic grayling. With it's long, flowing dorsal fin and subtle, purple, grey, and green and gold colorations of it's sides, grayling are a very striking specie, indeed, a specie seemingly created especially with the dry fly fisherman in mind.

Thymallus arcticus, or "sail fish of the north," or Arctic grayling are supposed to give off a faint odor of Thyme. However, since I seldom sniff fish,

Arctic grayling, or, 'Aristocrat of the North.' Flowing dorsal fin (more prominent on males) is most distinguishing characteristic. Grayling have been shown to live to remarkably old ages. The Alaska record grayling weighed 4 pounds 13 ounces.

especially a gift fish, I couldn't say for certain. Actually that's a lie. Once, at Crescent Lake in the Kenai's, I did try sniffing a grayling—but the look of my fishing companion's face when I did so made me quit immediately—and I've failed to attempt repeating the procedure ever since.

It is commonly believed that grayling 'take' flies at the surface on their way back down after jump-

ing. I'm not sure if this is always the case, but I do know there are many times that this seems to be what happens. Often it's hard to tell for certain, since grayling can take dry flies so quickly. What makes grayling especially fun for a fly fisher is that they're usually a very hungry fish, and therefore not entirely difficult to catch. Grayling are a great for beginning, intermediate, or advanced

61

dry fly fishermen, alike.

Arctic grayling and dark dry flies (like a Black Gnat or a Griffith's Gnat) are all but synonymous in Alaska, but any number of size-14, or size-16 dry flies will take grayling all day long, the only fly in the ointment (pun not intended) being that the fisherman might have to switch sizes now and then... just to keep things interesting for the fish.

My favorite grayling fly might surprise some anglers. It's a size-12 Griffith's Gnat (yes, a size-12) tied with a peacock herl body and a wisp of white hackle palmered along the length of the body. This pattern is deadly on grayling. Pinch the barb down on one of these babies and I guarantee you can catch grayling all day long—IF, of course, you're standing in good grayling water, and—IF you'll adapt to a smaller size fly now and then when the fishing begins to go 'stale' after an hour or two.

Arctic grayling can be taken in many places across Alaska, with the exceptions being the southeast 'panhandle,' the Kenai Peninsula, and Kodiak Island. Nome and points east and north are prime, old-country grayling habitat with many premier grayling waters offering some real giants. The flow between the Ugashik Lakes in the southwest part of the state is generally considered The Great Land's most-respected grayling fishery. Lake Clark country is also revered for its' grayling habitat, and I know of one

Nanci Morris shows the enjoyment that goes with arctic grayling dry fly fishing. This typical grayling was fooled by a Black Gnat imitation on the surface.

particular stream there that's so good the guide that took made me swear on a stack of Alaska State Fishing Regulations that I'd never reveal the secret.

Alaska's Ugashik Lakes region is usually considered Arctic grayling 'Holy Water.'

The first time I fished there I took a 21-inch grayling on my first cast - *and they say a 20" grayling in Alaska is considered a legitimate trophy of a lifetime.*

Brant Bunous, my companion on a trip to the Alaska Peninsula, also took a number of 20-plus inch grayling, along with one surefire 22-inch giant during that trip. We estimated Brant's big grayling would definitely weigh something over four pounds. I'm not sure about the age of that fish, but I swear it looked older than I am.

Needless to say, we returned those huge, old graybacks to their native haunts. Hopefully they're still there today, still finning their same, familiar currents as this is written, a couple of years later.

I still get a case of the shudders every time I hold my hands apart for someone to show how big Brant's grayling really was. *Really.* For all we know, that grayling might have been the new world's record.

I guess we'll never really know for certain..

Arctic grayling are usually

This large, old 21-inch grayling was released immediately after photo was taken. Hopefully this monster is alive and larger than ever today, and still finning it's same, familiar currents. Photo by Brant Bunous.

found in ice cold, crystal clear water. The clearer and colder the better, it seems. True, sometimes grayling *are* found finning silty seams in glacial rivers, (usually feasting on a salmon egg extravaganza) but as a rule grayling seek-out the purest, quinine-clear waters.

If you've never caught grayling on a fly rod until your wrists ache and your arms feel ready to drop off, you haven't experienced one of Alaska's pure fly fishing joys. Mark Bell of *High Adventure Air,* of Soldotna, recently flew Evan Swensen and me to a spot he knows of near Iliamna that easily surpassed any other grayling fishery I've ever had the pleasure of experiencing. I couldn't believe that such a river exists. It was like dying and going to grayling heaven for a day. We didn't see another fisherman all day and the stream we fished was so astonishingly clear that it was difficult to negotiate our footing because we couldn't make-out the water's depth. I've seldom fished in water that clear anywhere in my life, just as I've never caught grayling in numbers like that before, either. Ironically, this trip was the only time I ever had the pleasure of fishing with Mr. Swensen.

I'll be scheduling another day trip for Arctic grayling with *High Adventure Air* to that Arctic Grayling Dream Stream again this coming season—I can assure you.

A common dilemma Alaska's fly fishermen must face is the choice of deciding whether to cast for grayling or rainbows in many of Alaska's optimum dry fly waters.

I faced this challenge the first time I ever waded out in the lovely Agulawok. To be honest, I never really knew if my first cast there was for grayling or for rainbows. All I knew was there were so many fish surfacing all around us that I'd better get a fly out there for something to grab, and in a hurry. That something, in the form of my first fish taken from my first cast on the 'Wok, turned out to be a beautiful, 18-inch grayling. The wait must have taken six or seven seconds for that first fish. After a dozen or so grayling I began to calm down a bit and finally started concentrating on rainbows.

The best months to fly fish for grayling are: late May and two weeks into June, and then again in September and October. But, that doesn't preclude an angler from finding excellent grayling fishing during the other summer months, also.

*The official Alaska state record for arctic grayling is listed at 4 pounds, 13 ounces, but I know of a number of individuals who swear they've caught larger. (When an angler routinely releases fish it's difficult to know for certain).

Next time you feel like getting away from it all, try a fly-out fly fishing trip with arctic grayling in mind. Chances are you'll be flown to a pristine, virgin stream that you can have all to yourself. There you can often catch and release one of God's finest creations ...the Arctic grayling....on a dry fly... all day long.

All the while you can be trying your hardest to decide... for once and for all....if grayling take a fly on *their way up,... or on their way back down.* ⟜🦟

*Fly fisher Brant Bunous with the largest grayling
the author has ever seen. This fish wasn't weighed, but it
measured over 22 inches...a new world record? We'll never know
for sure. Brant quickly released the fish after photo was taken.*

*Dan Heiner with an 8 pound Rainbow
taken while fishing at Dennis McCracken's
Copper River Lodge at Iliamna.*

RAINBOW TROUT

ALASKA'S PREMIER SPORTFISH

L ike many anglers who spend a fair amount of time fly fishing *The Great Land*, for some reason I usually associate fly fishing Alaska with fishing for Alaska's rainbow trout. Naturally, like other fly rodders who call Alaska home, I spend some of my time fly fishing for Dollies and steelhead, for sockeyes and silvers, for grayling and arctic char.

However, if I'm honest with myself, it's Alaska's rainbows that I'm really chasing. In the end, most of my fly fishing hopes and dreams tend to revolve around Alaska's beautiful, heavily-spotted rainbow trout.

To this day I find myself dreaming (including day dreams) about many of the Alaska rainbows I've had the pleasure of meeting up close and personal over the past few years.

Rainbow trout have a way of gaining a fly fisherman's full attentions.

Some of these 'bows have not been huge by any means, going only around five pounds or so, while others have weighed ten to twelve, and there have been quite a few in between. All of these rainbows have formed vivid, lasting memories in my mind.

Rainbow trout seem to have a way of doing that ...

Every once in a while I'll run into another fly fisherman who has just recently taken up the sport. On more than one occasion I've had individuals question my affinity for rainbow trout over Alaska's other species.

"What makes rainbow fishing so good?" they'll ask, or, "Don't you get excited about fishing for silver salmon or kings?"

Invariably, my answer is the same, and for the life of me, I don't mean it to sound like I'm one of those "purists" who must fish rainbows on a dry fly at the surface or nothing at all. Here's what I say, and *you* be the judge if it sounds sanctimonious or not:

"I'd rather catch a ten-inch rainbow than a ten-pound salmon, any day of the week."

That's not a chop to salmon—it's simply a reflection of the magic rainbow trout fly fishing offers.

Some of the rainbows I have taken were hooked on egg-patterns as they hovered below schools of milling sockeye salmon, while some have been hooked as they sipped at dry flies at the surface of gin-clear Alaska rivers. At various times I've also relied on streamers like an Egg-Sucking Leech or a black and brown, 'Woolly Bugger' to provoke some dramatic, hard-hitting strikes.

Frank Plunk, owner of Big Mountain Lodge, *with typical Lower Talarik Creek 5-pound rainbow. The majority of rainbows at Alaska's premier sport fisheries are released, just one of the reasons these waters continue to produce year after year.*

These, and a black "Electric-Leech," (a Woolly Bugger tied with flashabou in it's tail) have enticed some memorable fish and some line-jarring hits.

Once in a while I find myself thinking about the seven pounder I encountered at 'the cut bank' at Brooks River, that big 'buck' (or male) with one eye missing. That old veteran grabbed my black Electric Leech pattern so hard it almost yanked the fly rod from my hand...

When one stops to consider that only about one in seventeen bazillion anglers (nationwide) ever gets the opportunity of hooking into a rainbow trout that actually weighs *over* 10 pounds, it tends to make a fly fisherman begin to appreciate how good he's had it (or has it) depending upon whether he lives in Alaska, or not. It shouldn't surprise anyone too much that there are a number of fly fishermen who make Alaska their home year round primarily because of the fantastic fly fishing found here.

During the winters we write books about fly fishing...

Those memories of rainbow trout on a fly rod that have weighed 8 to 10 pounds (some of them taken on dry flies) can live with a fly fisher forever. *...In full, living color.*

At the outlet of famed Lake Iliamna, at a river named Kvichak, (pronounced Kwee-Jack) an angler stands an excellent chance of hooking a rainbow trout that can weigh up to 18 or 20 pounds. For those (like me) who might be a little hard of hearing or a little hard to convince, let me repeat that, again, if I may:

I said,...Eighteen to twenty pound rainbows!

I could hardly believe my eyes the day Frank Plunk (co-owner of *Big Mountain Lodge* on the Kvichak) lifted a frozen, 37-inch rainbow from the lodge freezer and held it up for me to photograph. Seems an angler from out of state had gone fishing with *Big Mountain Lodge* co-owner John Hutchinson and had hooked into a monster rainbow. Apparently, when they finally got a glimpse of the size of the fish, the client couldn't bring himself to release it - and it ended up in the lodge freezer on it's way to a taxidermist. That rainbow had weighed something close to eighteen pounds when caught. I'd have liked to have been there to catch a glimpse of that angler's eyes as he focused on the size of that

rainbow as they lifted it in the net. It probably looked a lot like a fairly large king coming out of the water.

For those who might not know it, The Kvichak River is considered by many knowledgeable sportsmen to be *the* Alaska river producing the largest rainbows in the state.

Maybe, maybe not.

There are streams surrounding Lake Iliamna that, at the right time of year, also hold some extremely large rainbows - monster 'bows, they're called. Frank Plunk and I spent three glorious days sampling many of these streams a year or so ago by hopping around in Frank's Piper Super Cub. It shouldn't surprise anyone who's experienced it that my memories of that week in the Iliamna area remain as some of the extraordinary fly fishing of my life.

For years, Alaska's

The author with a 7-pound rainbow taken at Brooks River. This fish took a black, 'Electric Leech" pattern so energetically it nearly tore the rod from author's hands. Photo by Chuck Lickhalter.

Kukaklek and Nonvianuk Lakes have been among Alaska's strongholds for producing trophy rainbows. The Alagnak, (also called *The Branch River*) is so named because of the convergence of the two drainages of Nonvianuk and Kukaklek Lakes. As one can easily imagine, the culmination (the Alagnak River) becomes a premier rainbow fishery, a virtual rainbow heaven.

Not to be confused with *Angler's Paradise*, but close.

Alaska *on the Fly*

Fueled, primarily, by the numbers of fish in the sockeye salmon runs each year, rainbows will follow the fertile salmon for miles in every direction as they gorge on the loose, drifting eggs. Then, late in the summer, after the salmon have spawned and die and start to decay, the rainbows switch to the taking of drifting salmon flesh, which begins to swirl back downstream, playing-out nature's method of refertilizing the entire drainage and ecosystem.

It's no secret that the rainbow trout is *The* Alaska fish in the eyes of most bonafide, dyed-in-the-wool fly fishermen. Why? Well, for one thing, rainbows don't just jump, they generally *rocket* from the water's surface, providing electrifying action for the fly rodder. If you haven't had a five pound or larger 'bow hook itself at the surface on *your* size-14 dry fly, then flip over, cartwheel in mid air a couple of times, and plunge back into currents - you simply haven't experienced one of Alaska's *crem de 'la crem* fly fishing experiences.

It's a good thing my wife understands life's major priorities...

John Hutchinson of Big Mountain Lodge *with a "small," 5-pound rainbow taken while drifting the Kvichak (pronounced Kwee-Jack) at the outlet of Lake Iliamna.*

One of the beauties of fly fishing for rainbows is, the angler never seems to get tired of the thrills involved in hooking and playing these 'hot-blooded' fish.

This past season I had the opportunity of spending ten days fly fishing Alaska with nationally-acclaimed fishing and outdoor writer, John Gierach. It was John's first visit to Alaska, and it was my distinct pleasure to welcome him to The Great Land.

As I recall, one of the first rainbows John hooked on our trip was a six pounder he took on the surface of Iliamna's Copper River using a size-14 dry fly, a *Western Adams* if I remember correctly. Even though John had caught and released hundreds of rainbows in his life prior to hooking that Alaskan beauty, he grinned like a schoolboy with his very first fish when that big 'bow grabbed his fly, bent-over his pretty, little 5-weight bamboo rod, and catapulted up through the surface in a head-shaking blast.

Then, a few minutes later and a few hundred yards downstream, a five pounder made me a believer, too, by tucking *my* size-12 Irresistible in the corner of it's mouth and stripping backing from my reel as though it wasn't about to stop until it reached Pedro Bay. As usual, I found myself whooping and hollering as if it were my first rainbow taken on a dry fly.

Excited? Not us. Not in the slightest...

But, it's when you can actually see those big, heavily-spotted rainbows with their dark, British Racing Green backs and crimson pinstripes as they're sipping naturals at the surface or hovering just below, or, better yet, when they're finning, *just there in the currents,* looking entirely 'catchable'.... that can really raise an angler's eyebrows. That's when your blood pressure begins to rise, your pulse quickens, your eyes widen, and your casting arm begins an uncontrollable twitch.

I won't soon forget the first time I fished at lovely *Wood River Lodge* in the Wood River/Tikchik Lakes region in southwestern Alaska. The river we were at looked for all the world like we'd died and gone to rainbow, grayling, and char heaven - *all in one.* Fish of all sizes and species were rising to naturals all around

us. It was just like I had always imagined fly fishing utopia would be like - ever since I began dreaming about rainbow trout on a full time basis some years ago.

It wasn't good... *it was great!* What's that? A drift WITH-OUT a fish? No way! ... Don't go kidding me!

One thing's for certain: It *would* be extremely difficult to have to choose just one of Alaska's premier rainbow fisheries over all others. Heaven

Moment of truth for Copper River rainbow trout. Originally thought to be about a 4-pounder when first hooked, this fish turned out to be closer to eight! Notice clarity of the water.

knows I've been terribly fortunate to have had the opportunity of visiting some of Alaska's finest fishing lodges over the past five or six years.

Every Alaska fly fisher tends to form his or her own "scrapbook" of great experiences, but I would have a particularly difficult decision before me if someone were to inform me, "..Okay, we're going to let you relive one, and *only* one of your greatest rainbow experiences. Which one will it be?"

I'd have to think on that one for a while.

Wood River Lodge in the Tikchik Lakes region would be *'a given.'* Like I say, I still find myself dreaming about the dry fly water found there.

Dennis McCracken's *Copper River Lodge* also comes to mind in a heartbeat, too. As anyone who's fished *the Copper* can tell you, that river has a way of making rainbow fishermen out of salmon anglers in a hurry. It's simple, really: Just go out as a salmon angler for sockeyes in the morning, and by the time you stop for lunch you'll have realized you've been promoted to the ranks of veteran rainbow fanatic. Those six, seven, and eight pound Copper River 'bows with their bright pinkish-red racing stripes are enough to make a salmon angler forget what he came to Alaska for in the first place. Take a look at the nearly 8-pounder I'm holding on page 66 of this book if you'd like a better idea of what the rainbows at Iliamna's *Copper River* look like.

Terese Blair ready to release rainbow while float tube fishing.

Or, maybe the one, premier day of fly fishing for rainbows for me to experience again would be the day that Tom Bukowski and I landed at that wild, remote, unnamed, Iliamna river where I managed to hook and land nearly a dozen trophy 'bows, the largest weighing something approaching twelve pounds. That was the day that Tom personally caught and released over twenty monster rainbows, himself, and then later told me about the brown bear that had stood watching from behind me for something like ten minutes, sniffing intently as I innocently cast to a group of circling rainbows—*bandits I call 'em*— each of them looking larger in diameter than one of my thighs.

Those rainbows were hovering like a group of hungry piranhas below a swarming school of sockeyes that had congregated in that gin-clear wilderness pool. The water in that stream was so entirely clear that it was nearly invisible at times. Occasionally I'd make a mistake and step into a pool far deeper than I'd thought it to be.

Tom said he'd have shouted to scare that bear away except that I'd looked so consumed with my fishing that he didn't have the heart to disturb me - *not just then, anyway.* He said the bear had looked for all the world like a 'big 'ol 10-foot Teddy' standing there,' watching me from behind as I cast, drifted the egg-pattern, and cast again.

I never even knew that bear existed. But, even if I *had*, I probably wouldn't have minded much, not at that moment, anyway. Any second now, a giant *rainbow of a lifetime* could have peeled out of the pack and intercepted my drifting egg pattern - and all of a sudden BE THERE - all in one incredible instant!

I thought maybe I'd died and gone to rainbow heaven...

But, then again, just possibly the *one* evening of fly fishing I'd like to relive all over again would be the evening Bob Singer and I got our first taste of phenomenal *Kulik,* with its hundreds of beautiful, spotted rainbows...*at the surface.* Neither Bob or I could believe what our eyes and our bent fly rods were telling us. Scream-ers!... at the surface... and on *Dry Flies.*

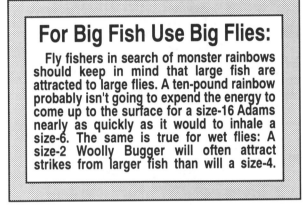

For Big Fish Use Big Flies:

Fly fishers in search of monster rainbows should keep in mind that large fish are attracted to large flies. A ten-pound rainbow probably isn't going to expend the energy to come up to the surface for a size-16 Adams nearly as quickly as it would to inhale a size-6. The same is true for wet flies: A size-2 Woolly Bugger will often attract strikes from larger fish than will a size-4.

I knew Nonvianuk was good, but the fish-ing was so phenomenal that for a minute or two there I felt like we were fishing back in 1953 and we were the only anglers who'd ever set foot at the place.

Maybe they call Katmailand *Anglers Paradise* for a reason?

Bob and I still talk about that evening and those rainbows. And, yes, I was out there whooping and hollering , as usual, while those rainbows performed their aerial antics.

Kulik Manager Bo Bennett had told us we'd enjoy the fishing.

Both Bo, and Katmailand's owner, Raymond 'Sonny' Petersen are ex-tremely experienced pilots and guides who know this part of Alaska as well as anyone. Sonny's father, Raymond Petersen, Sr., (co-founder of the operation back in the late 40's along with Johnny Walatka) named *Angler's Paradise Lodges* very appropriately, I can assure you.

But I can't forget my first experience over on the Alagnak, at Bobby DeVito's *Branch River Lodge,* either. A group of the guides had gathered down at the dock after supper for some casual chat and fishing, so Dad and I stretched our legs after dinner and walked down and joined them.

Seems the resident rainbows were going crazy, gorging themselves on salmon entrails discarded into the river by a couple of the guides who were finishing-up cleaning the day's king salmon catch. It's the kind of habit 'local 'bows' get into in many places across Alaska. Almost in disbelief, Dad and I watched the feeding frenzy.

Any number of monster rainbows could be seen shooting up, out of the river's depths, viciously attacking the offerings as they drifted downstream in the currents. Those rainbows, seemingly numbering in the hundreds, appeared to be everything from three to twelve pounders, looking for all the world like a school of starved piranhas as they ripped voraciously at the drifting entrails.

Fortunately, I happened to have "'ol lucky" with me, my old 8 1/2 foot, 8-weight Orvis bamboo fly rod I'd picked up from Len Codella a year or two earlier. Thinking I might try my luck a bit as we kidded with the guides, I worked out some floating line and began lengthening-out a cast...and drifted a single egg pattern.. a little pinkie...out there... just... like... WHAM!!

Dennis McCracken, owner of Copper River Lodge, *with a nice 6-pound 'bow taken on a peach-colored 'Glo-Bug,,' a single-egg pattern.*

A rainbow (it looked to be about a 4 1/2 pounder, about a 24-incher) grabbed the 'pinkie' almost as it neared the end of it's drift. Before I knew it, the fish shot up through the surface, and hung there, shimmering in the air. For a moment it seemed frozen in animation, with my fly line and leader leading directly to it's lower lip. Almost in disbelief, we watched as the rainbow began to cartwheel down, smacking hard on the wooden dock with a solid thud! There it remained - *motionless.*

No one could believe what had happened. I was as surprised as anyone. Dad and I ran over to where the fish lay. Ever so carefully I lifted the beautiful rainbow from the dock.

The fish was still alive, but definitely dazed and in shock. A perfect, wet impression remained on the dock where the rainbow had crash landed. Ironically, it was one of the prettiest rainbows I've ever laid my eyes on, typical

74

of Kukaklek system fish. That subspecies has a deep, almost-transparent, somewhat iridescent blue green look to them that is difficult to describe and somewhat different than any other rainbows I've ever had the pleasure of meeting up close and personal. It's also a very heavily spotted rainbow subspecies.

If you get the feeling I like Kukaklek/Nonvianuk rainbows you're right.

The others hurried over to get a closer look, too. Slowly, the dazed rainbow began to move slightly. Carefully cradling the fish in my hands, I gently lowered it back into the river's currents. Eventually it began to move its gills and take-in oxygen. I continued to hold it in the currents for what seemed like fifteen minutes while it regained it's strength.

Finally, Dad nodded that the rainbow was ready to be released and I loosened my grasp. When I did, the spotted beauty swam casually away, disappearing into the river's depths, as though nothing out of the ordinary had ever happened.

For a moment we all stood there, looking at the river in silence and disbelief.

I had practiced catch and release before, but that rainbow had given a whole new meaning to the word...

I suppose any reflection on Alaska's great rainbow waters wouldn't be complete if it didn't include some famous streams like the Copper, the 'Wood River' in the Tikchik Lakes chain, or world-reknown 'Lower Talarik Creek,' with its famous 'rock hole' just 15 minutes away by Super Cub from Big Mountain Lodge at the outlet of Iliamna.

Of course, the Newhalen, at Iliamna is also a particular favorite of many, *yours truly included.* Over King Salmon way, the Naknek River would have to be included, too. And, it just wouldn't be right to go overlooking that storybook of storybook rivers, the Brooks, located at Katmai Park.

But then there are those outstanding tributaries in nearly every direction from Iliamna that can jump out and grab an angler's attention *real fast.* To the west, the Togiak, Goodnews, and the Kanektok Rivers are particularly famous rainbow producers. It all adds up to the kind of angling that makes fly fishermen addicted to the sport, some of the very best in all of North America.

Decisions, decisions...

Actually, after all is said and done it *would* be extremely difficult for anyone to have to pick out *one* river over all others as being Alaska's premier rainbow trout stream. There are so many great rainbow fisheries in Alaska that it's hard to fathom one as being superior to the others.

But it sure is fun to dream about...

As soon as you get to thinking you've learned the ultimate Alaska rainbow stream another will suddenly emerge and stare you in the face... and begin stealing your affections.

The Alaska state record Rainbow/Steelhead is listed as a 42 pound, 3 ouncer taken in 1970 off Bell Island. That sounds a lot like a misprint to many, and sounds like a whopping steelhead to me, either a granddaddy of a fish, or the world's record misprint - I'm not sure which. But, in Alaska it IS always good to remember that... fact IS often stranger than fiction.

Remember: do yourself, the fish, and Alaska a favor: Always pinch the barbs down on your flies and release all the rainbow trout you catch in Alaska. Contrary to what some visitors may tell you, Alaska's rainbows ARE NOT a never-ending resource...unless we make them that way by killing them. **If you are not in the habit of practicing catch and release fly fishing, try it on your next trip. I guarantee, you'll enjoy your fishing more with every fish that you watch swim away -** *after* you've had a friend snap a picture of you with your trophy, of course!

Author with stunning, 11-pound rainbow trout caught and released on Branch River tributary using an 8-weight rod. Photo by Tom Bukowski, Wild Rivers.

Monster 'bows

I f I were a confirmed trophy rainbow fly fisher who *had* to have fish over eight pounds or nothing at all (I'm not, I'm entirely happy to settle for 5-pounders at the surface on a dry fly any 'ol day) I would strongly consider the following waters for finding Alaska's huge rainbow trout:

Kvichak River —The Outlet of Lake Iliamna: (Pronounced Kwee-Jack) Rainbows 5 to 20 pounds, possibly the largest in the state. Deep water drifting, high-density sinking lines a "must." Rainbows up to thirty-seven plus inches - if you can imagine such a thing.

The Kenai River: Premier Alaska rainbow trout habitat - a steady producer year after year, fish in the 8 to 15 pound class. Check regulations carefully.

The Kenai River below Skilak Lake: Seven to ten miles of deep water and big rainbows. Pro-

Frank Plunk displays a frozen, 37-inch, 17 1/2-pound rainbow taken from Kvichak River near Big Mountain Lodge. The client that caught this trophy couldn't bring himself to release it.

duces some exceptionally large, trophy rainbows each year. Special 'Mid-River' drifts are available through guide services like *Great Alaska Fish Camp,* in Sterling, Alaska.

The Newhalen River: below the falls to Lake Iliamna: One of the most productive fisheries in the state - big water - excitement in the form of huge rainbows can happen at most unexpected times. Easy accessibility from nearby Iliamna Airport. This phenomenon called The Newhalen River is one of my favorites.

The Naknek River: Wild, powerful rainbows in this area of Alaska go for gaudy streamers, especially 'Buggers' like 'Black Electric Leech' and large Egg-Sucking Leeches. Watch for terrific, line-jarring strikes, especially 'on the swing.' Deep drifting from boats can be exceptional.

The Kukaklek / Nonvianuk Systems: There are many who believe the rainbows in the Kukaklek/Nonvianuk system are among the prettiest in the state, and I'm not about to argue. Must catch and release these rainbows to appreciate their beautiful, iridescent colors. Kulik Lodge (one of Alaska's premier rainbow spots) is located at the headwaters of this great drainage. Outstanding dry fly fishing. Downstream, the Alagnak (or Branch River) is superb rainbow habitat. Check with Bob DeVito, Jr. at Branch River Lodge about best times for super 'bows. Of course, Brooks River, situated just a few miles away from Nonvianuk

Mid September, when the temperature drops, is great time for large rainbows like this beauty caught and released while fishing at Copper River Lodge. Photo by Dennis McCracken.

Lake, is one of the premier rainbow trout streams in the state. Ask Brook Lodge Manager, Perry Mollan, to give the best techniques of how to go after the monsters at Brooks River.

Wood River/Tikchik Lakes Area: I still dream about these rivers on a regular basis. Some of the prettiest dry fly water in Alaska. Wade and cast dry flies, and fish while drifting downstream to lake systems - and fish lake mouths. Wood River Lodge is one of my all-time favorite Alaska fishing lodges.

Western Alaska Rivers: Togiak, Goodnews River, Kanektok, et. al: Last season I had to turn down two separate trips to both the Goodnews and the Kanektok because of work obligations back in Anchorage. When are they ever going to learn that Alaska should be shut down completely in summer so people can go fishing and take care of it's visitors? Contact Ron Hyde, Sr. or Ron Hyde, Jr. at *Alaska River Safaris* for combination fishing or rainbow fishing *extraordinare at its finest* at the Goodnews River, one of Alaska's exceptional fisheries.

Iliamna's Wild Rivers: Includes a number of exceptional, medium and small streams. Timing is of the utmost importance in finding success. Rivers in this area of state will provide anglers at any experience level with the ultimate Alaska remote country fly fishing experiences. Success requires knowledgeable lodge/guides, and expert pilot for access to inaccessible locations. These remote, wild rivers can contain very large rainbows at right times of year.

If optimum-sized rainbows are the desired goal, the Kvichak or Newhalen Rivers would probably be good places to start. However, fishing either of these two spots is best accomplished from a boat - (they're both big, deep water fisheries) although there are places where an angler can wade and really enjoy himself. Sometimes a fly fisher can get away

Tom Bukowski of Wild Rivers *made the front cover of* Alaska Outdoors *magazine with this beautiful rainbow. Tom caught and released over twenty trophies like this one this day.*

with casting from the islands, rocks, or sandbars, or further downstream, near where the currents widen. Should a fisherman hook a monster that turns and heads for deep water - all I could say would be,

"Best of Luck. Hope your tippet's got some strength!"

The Copper River at Iliamna certainly qualifies as a 'monster 'bow' alternative, too. There's no reason an angler couldn't find himself hooked into a monster at the lovely Copper - just like those fish in the pictures at Dennis McCracken's *Copper River Lodge.*

Concerning tackle for monster 'bows, go with the rod that you believe in, one that has enough backbone to (A) cast large, streamers and weighted flies and heavy, high-density sink-tip lines, and (B) be a rod with enough line weight to withstand Alaska's winds. I'd want a rod with at least the muscle of an 8-weight, or even a 9-weight, just in case I did happen to hook into a fifteen-plus pound fish or run into a gusty day. Many will say 6-weights or 7-weights are about right, but these are the same people who haven't seen or fished the Kvichak or the Newhalen yet. Having a reel with a stout drag might become appreciated in a hurry, also.

I sure wish Dad could have been with me the day I caught that twelve pounder...

NORTHERN PIKE

T he northern pike is the 'dragster' of the fish family," is how I once heard a young fishing guide describe **Esox lucius** to a client. I must admit, somehow that description seems to fit pike ... very well, indeed. These cagey, yellow and green-camouflaged *northerns* lie hidden in their weedy domains until something edible-looking disturbs the water surface and triggers a pike's strike mechanisms. Then, watch out! When

northern pike switch on their afterburners they're fully committed, and like a sidewinder missile, pike are on track to their target until they sink their hundreds (literally) of razor-sharp teeth

Northern pike are known for their sudden, explosive strikes at the surface. Photo by Evan Swensen

into their victim and twist it down to a watery grave. It's said that ducklings and goslings are in grave danger while swimming in pike country, and if this is true, then it follows that mice and muskrats probably wouldn't want to spend much time worrying about their old age insurance, either.

Alaska is loaded with good pike fishing waters. Where? Often, most anywhere between point A and point B. All those unnamed lakes out on Alaska's tundras are likely spots for finding pike, provided there is some type of flow present to aerate the water. If it looks like it should harbor pike, chances are good they're there.

The most talked about pike country in Alaska is the Minto Flats region near

Fairbanks, but don't count out discovering pike at many of Alaska's hundreds of other slackwater areas. In fact, northern pike can be found in over 80% of Alaska's areas.

Although pike are pure fun to fish for using a fly rod, I don't know anyone who takes pike fishing too seriously, although it makes for great sport, and from what I hear, the popularity of pike fishing is on the rise. Many times, salmon and char rivers will feature stillwater offshoots or canals that hold pike, and sometimes some very large specimens, indeed.

For a break in the action from the regular fishing out in the faster currents, try tossing a large, colorful, gaudy-looking streamer over near the water lilies in the slower water estuaries - where pike are likely to be waiting for one form or another of innocent prey. Retrieve the fly on the surface by stripping in quick, jerky movements. Nothing works better than a mouse imitation on the surface, so get ready for quick action when using one of these deadly patterns. It usually happens quickly or it doesn't happen at all. Sometimes a second cast employing slower strips will trigger a fish that might have been caught napping when the first 'meal' slipped by.

Although the initial strike of a northern pike is sudden, pike are not especially renowned for offering prolonged, deliberate battles. Smaller pike are extremely numerous in many waters and are referred to as, "Hammer Handles."

Anglers will want to wear gloves and use pliers when removing hooks from pikes' mouths.

Northern pike, or "Hammer Handle" like this are great fun to catch on a fly rod. Deer-hair mice and long, colorful streamers stripped at the surface will entice strikes.

For those desiring good pike fishing close to Anchorage, Hewitt Lake, near Skwentna, is great pike country, as are the series of lakes to be found above the Yentna near where Lake Creek enters. Check with John Logan at Skwentna Roadhouse and Fishing Lodge for additional information regarding this part of Alaska.

Scott Horn, a friend who's fly fished Southcentral Alaska extensively, recently revealed his favorite method of catching pike. One day, Scott said,, while he was hurrying to motor across a small pike-filled-lake in a small boat, he inadvertently allowed a colorful, long-shanked streamer to drag in the wake behind the boat. Suddenly, out of nowhere, a large pike struck and hooked itself, causing Scott to grab for his fishing rod to keep it from flipping overboard. It wasn't until then that Scott realized he'd hooked a pike. Later, on another trip, Scott tried the same tactic again and experienced the same results. Proclaiming it was great sport, Scott began to realize that best results in hook-ups improved the faster he cranked his little 3-H.P. motor. Soon, whether the fishing had been any good that day or not, Scott found himself 'trolling' for pike on his way back home. Not exactly classic fly fishing, *but interesting,* and definitely food for thought.

Dad and I found excellent northern pike fishing at many of White Mountain's Fish River still-water offshoots and sloughs a few years ago. I bet Dad I could catch a pike larger than anything he could muster, but there's no reason to belabor the outcome of that bet just now. Suffice it to say Dad's pike was *slightly* larger than mine, if ten pounds qualifies as slightly larger.

The entire contest lasted about seven minutes.

Many pike 'experts' expound on how necessary wire leaders are for taking pike, but it's been my experience that using 20lb. or 25lb. monofilament leaders will usually handle a number of small northerns before chafing makes it necessary to change leaders.

Pike can make for excellent dining... *IF* they are filleted and baked right on the spot. I've enjoyed some tasty 'shore lunches' produced from fresh-caught northerns cooked over an

White Mountain fishing guide with medium northern pike taken from 'slack water area' away from river's main currents.

open fire. Try a little paprika and fresh-squeezed lemon, or sprinkle lemon garlic and butter next time you dine-out for **Esox lucius,** won't you! Be sure to invite the ladies to join-in, too.

Northern Pike are best located and fished for during the summer months of June, July, and August, and are found mostly in the northern two-thirds of the state. **The Alaska record for Northern Pike is a 38 pounder taken in '78 at Fish Creek.** Fishermen sometimes talk about waters containing forty-plus pound pike, but so far anyway, no one has accomplished the feat, at least not officially, anyway. However, the last thirty-pound pike I got a glimpse at looked so fierce as it eyed me from the shallows that I wouldn't want to be caught standing in the same water containing a forty-pounder.

Since pike are masters of survival, don't count out seeing them in waters where 'they're simply not supposed to be." Jim Salisbury, a good friend and fishing companion, even reported catching a glimpse of a pike in the slack waters of the Brooks River at Katmai last season.

Now... there's a northern pike with ...cl*ass!*

STEELHEAD: RAINBOWS WORTH THEIR SALT

To many fishermen (myself included) there's something exceedingly enticing and magical about hooking into a silver-dollar-bright, fresh from the ocean, saltwater-traveled rai*nbow trout* that measures something like 30 inches in length and weighs from seven to fourteen, or fifteen pounds.

It's fly fishing like this that has developed the respected breed of anglers known today as: *Steelheaders.*

Being a 'steelheader' is not an official title, but those who know of anglers in these circles (or better yet, actually know a real-life steelheader *personally*) know that being a 'steelheader' is not a title to be taken lightly. In fact, there are plenty of anglers who are willing to admit that being recognized as a, *steelheader,* is something to be revered, something akin to being knighted by the Queen, herself, or being honored at the annual fly fishing banquet by none other than the local president.

There's no doubt about it: Being a *steelheader* is serious stuff. You can spit into the wind, and you can even pull on the mask of the 'ol lone ranger, but you'd better not go messin' around with a weather-tempered.... *steelheader.*

Not surprisingly, **Oncorhynchus mykiss** *Oceanious* are typically among the most prestigious trophies any flyrodder worth his salt could ever covet. Steelhead are cold water creatures which, it is nearly universally agreed, almost always require stout, hardy anglers to catch them; real men from what is said, anglers who can be ready to go fishing at the drop of a hat and brave the elements, no matter how harsh they may be.

Any fisherman who'll gladly risk everything to hook into a fish that provides powerful, line-ripping runs coupled with acrobatic leaps *deserves* to be in a class by himself. *Steelheaders* are not only revered among their own - but, better yet, respected by society in general. These are fly fishers so impassioned that they can see it beginning to snow, drop whatever it is they are doing, grab the nearest fly rod and jump into the pickup and speed to the nearest steelhead river. Never mind if the wife has just started dinner and the kids are waiting at the schoolyard, or the fact that the nearest steelhead stream might be four hours away. Any dyed-in-the-wool steelheader must have his set of priorities and keep them straight.

Generally speaking, Alaska's steelhead are not as large as some of those found in some Canadian rivers like the famous Skeena system, which includes the famous Babine and the Kispiox. In Alaska, any 15-pound steelhead is a dandy, although 20-pounders DO get caught on occasion, many coming from southeast Alaska's Situk River near Yakutat. Once in a while a monster is taken from the Thorne River or nearby rivers on Prince of Wales Island across from Ketchikan.

I used to think that catching just one rose-plated steelhead in my lifetime would be all the magic I could ever ask for, but I've since learned that greed is as much a part of a steelheader's vices as it is that of a regular 'ol rainbow fisherman's. It's nearly impossible to invest the patience, devote the time and travel, or brave the elements for long to simply accept the thrill of catching only *one* steelhead in one's lifetime. Steelhead trout are simply too rare and too beautiful for a fly fisherman to be happy with catching ...just one .

Landing one's first steelhead on a fly rod makes for indelible memories, and I still find myself shaking my head whenever I think about my first experience. The place was Southcentral Alaska's Anchor River, a lovely little stream located near that 'end of the road' town, Homer, Alaska.

For years I'd heard the tales and seen the videos of anglers braving the elements and fishing for long hours to catch a steelhead. Naturally, I reasoned I'd have to devote many hours just to get a nibble, much less actually hook into and land one.

It was mid-September at the time, and I was fishing with Dr. Franklin (Doc) Smith, a companion I've shared numerous outdoor experiences with over the years. If I recall correctly, it was I who taught Doc how to shoot ducks over decoys years earlier, but that was *before* I learned about the thrills of fly fishing Alaska. Be that as it may, Doc accepted my offer to join me in Alaska. Three days later Doc flew up from 'the lower 48' to meet me, all ready to go.

It took us about four hours of steady driving just to get from to the river, so when we finally arrived I was anxious to begin fishing. Quickly I assembled my fly rod and walked over to have a 'look see' while Doc finished rigging-up his gear.

Reaching in my fly box, I pulled-out the first, single-egg pattern I came to, a "flame" colored, size-8 Glo-Bug. I tied it on as a 'searching' fly, a color I had never fished before in my life.

The hole directly in front of me looked fairly good, so, quickly I made a cast, allowing the egg-pattern to drift naturally through the riffles. Nothing happened so I picked-up the line and cast again...

On my second drift my fly line suddenly tightened. Lifting the rod I proceeded to set the hook on my very first steelhead! Before I knew it I was battling a ten or eleven pound beauty.

I had actually hooked a 30-plus inch steelhead trout on my second cast, ...

I felt almost guilty for hooking that fish. After all, *I* was the guy who was supposed to be the 'host.' *Doc* was supposed to be the fisherman.

Oh, well, sometimes we've gotta stop and smell the roses, as they say...right?

It took only a few more moments for me to realize that I actually had a Steelhead at the end of my line - a specie I had wanted to add to my 'list' of Alaskan species for many years.

Even 'small' steelhead (or sea-going rainbows) like this 6-pound fish are revered by most flyrodders. Anglers who specialize in saltwater rainbows are referred to as: Steelheaders. *Photo by Richard Chiappone.*

I was trying-out a new rod I'd picked up recently, a 9-foot, 7/8-weight, graphite II, IM-6 grapite fly rod I'd found on sale a few days earlier at a local sporting goods store. I needed that rod like I needed more stress in my life, but I bought it anyway—I had to: the price was just too good to refuse. However, it turned out to be lucky— and a perfect fly rod for the steelhead we encountered.

Presently Doc came running over, all excited. Doc's the kind of companion who enjoys the outdoors regardless of who's catching fish or "carrying the lucky horseshoe" any particular day.

Doc must have realized I was playing my first steelhead, and consequently, there wasn't enough he could do to assist me. Quickly, without speaking, he grabbed my camera from the front pouch of my waders and began snapping photos of me with the fish (figuring one of them might turn out) for posterity.

The steelhead's colors were just like the textbooks had said they would be: It's head and back were a dark, metalflake-plated, cobalt-blue in color. Combined with its' glistening, purplish-rosey colored gill plate, and it's stylish, streamlined body design, that steelhead made for quite a sight, indeed.

Instantly I realized why steelhead are so widely revered. Somehow, that fish seemed to have an aura of 'aristocracy' about it. I've since learned that all Steelhead do.

I don't think I'll ever forget the warm feeling I experienced of cradling that 30-inch steelhead in my hands in that beautiful, cold Alaskan stream. For a full five minutes or more I worked the beautiful fish back and forth in the shallows to help it regain oxygen before releasing it. My hands began to go numb in the cold water but that didn't matter. When Doc assured me the steelie had regained enough strength, I finally released it back to the hole I had caught it from.

"Go make some more Steelies!" I muttered.

Doc and I stood there for a few minutes staring at the riffles. Neither of us wanted to be the first to speak and somehow break the magic we felt at that moment. Standing there in silence, we listened to the sounds of the river and pondered the marvels of God's creations...

Finally I decided to bring things back to reality.

"Well, so much for those stories of long, tedious hours of fishing for Steelhead, Doc"...I said.

I knew I had been lucky that day - I just didn't know HOW lucky...

Neither of us could believe how kind the fishing gods had been to me that afternoon. Ironically, less than half an hour later, I was able to catch and release yet another steelhead, and then a fresh, bright, twelve-pound silver salmon. Both fish came quickly to a Brown and Black *Woolly Bugger* fished deep using a long, 10-foot Umpqua leader and a Wulff Triangle Taper, 8/9-weight floating line. I'd crimped-on a couple of 'split shot' down near the fly to get the fly down to where the fish would be found. A sink-tip line, such as a Teeny T-300 might have been a better choice, but ...like they say,...*all's well that end's well* .

I released the second steelhead like the first, but asked Doc if he'd take the salmon back to the family in the lower 48, and he kindly agreed.

Although I officially became "hooked" on steelhead fishing that day, I found myself having serious doubts about some of the steelhead stories I'd heard in the past. Did some anglers *really* have to devote all those many hours to hooking just one fish?

It wasn't until ten days later that I began to realize how seriously I had taken to flyrodding for steelhead trout. Rich Chiappone's invitation to join him for another go at it rung in my ears like words straight from the promised land. Before I knew it, Rich and I were on our way back down the Kenai Peninsula again.

Each of us caught a fish or two before it got too dark to fish anymore that evening, but the foot or two of snow we awoke to the next morning pretty-well signaled the end of our fly fishing for another year. Reluctantly we turned our attentions to motoring our way up the snowy highway to Anchorage.

Doc had been back home in the lower 48 for nearly a month when Andy Macleod called asking if I'd like to fly down to the Anchor with him for yet one more go at steelies before winter set in for good. Not wanting to leave a friend stranded in time of need, I met Andy at his Super Cub at Merrill Field in Anchorage.

We found ourselves with the river all to ourselves that afternoon, greeted only by spectacularly clear, late-Indian-summer weather. Everything was absolutely perfect except for one thing: thousands of clumps of frozen ice were drifting along the river's surface. Like miniature icebergs, the ice dramatically changed our hopes of successful fishing. We found it nearly impossible to make a cast that would slip between the pieces of floating ice, even though we both suspected steelhead were still present in good numbers just inches below our offerings.

I'd done my share of dry fly fishing before, but the ice had given a whole new meaning to the concept of fishing a fly 'on the surface. '

Later, after admitting fishing season had finally come to an end, and after thinking about steelhead fishing through that winter, I realized what a wonderful gift Mother Nature has given to fly fishers: somehow there can be nothing better than saving the best of the year's fly fishing for last.

I was beginning to realize how affected I had become with fly fishing for steelhead...

Steelhead are **anadromous,** meaning they migrate and exist in both fresh and salt water as part of their natural life cycles. Most anadromous fish species have a stronger preference for salt water during the major feeding and growth phases of their lives, and steelhead trout fit into this category. Dolly Varden char are anadromous, too.

Regardless of when steelhead enter freshwater (some enter in spring, others in autumn) **steelhead spawn in spring,** just like their freshwater counterparts, the rainbows do. In fact, it is speculated that steelhead trout were once simply 'regular' rainbows that somehow developed the ability to survive in both fresh and salt water. Perhaps it had something to do with an ice age. Maybe a glacier formed, cutting off a subspecies of rainbow's return to freshwater? Who knows?

It is said that rainbows and steelhead are identical, except for the steelheads' ability to survive in the salt. The story goes that steelhead got their name from commercial fishermen, who had a tough time killing them by clubbing them over their heads: thus 'Steelhead.'

Because of the sea's vast food supplies, steelhead frequently grow to much larger sizes than do freshwater rainbows, which must pick from the scanty offerings available in fresh water compared to that of the sea.

Alaska has more than it's share of excellent steelhead streams, but with a human population geared mainly to both a private and a commercial salmon harvest, and a guiding network built and established primarily around the five species of Pacific salmon, steelhead fishing/guiding is still a largely untapped market/service in Alaska.

Consequently, many of Alaska's remote, premier steelhead rivers remain all but totally unexplored. Prince of Wales' Island, for example, features many little-understood steelhead streams that very few people even know the names of. One of the best known is the Thorne River, home of famed Boardwalk *Lodge*, where anglers may opt to fish either the deeper salt water for salmon or halibut, or explore some of the area's many steelhead and cutthroat waters, of which, perhaps only a dozen have been "explored." The Karta is another respected Prince of Wales Island steelhead river.

Waterfall Resort, at the other end of Prince of Wales Island caters primarily to saltwater fishermen, but I'm willing to bet some anglers wouldn't have to talk too awfully long or hard to get one or two of Waterfall's guides to take them on a *Steelie Safari.*

Some of Alaska's Best-Known Steelhead Fisheries are:
(1) Situk River near Yakutat
(2) Prince of Wales Island off Ketchikan
(3) Kodiak Island
(4) Kenai Peninsula, near Homer, Alaska

Although there is fantastic steelhead fishing to be found in Alaska in late April and in May, for many anglers steelhead fly fishing brings to mind memories of vivid fall colors and the chill of autumn air. If it's a particularly cold day the angler will have to spend some time attempting to maintain some degree of personal body heat. But let him hook into a steelhead and it's strange how all thoughts of keeping warm are quickly forgotten. Steelhead have a way of raising an angler's adrenaline levels very quickly. With a beautiful, ocean-fed rainbow weighing between seven and fifteen pounds at the end of his line, chances are good the fly fisher will feel the heat of excitement - *in a hurry.*

The Alaska record Steelhead weighed 42 pounds, 3 oz., a real anomaly, since relatively few 20 pounders are taken in Alaska annually. Most steelhead average around 8 or 9 pounds. The optimum steelhead fly rod is probably an 8-weight , or better yet, a light 9-weight fly rod of today's modern

Dan Heiner with a nice steelhead taken with a 7/8-weight rod, floating line, and a 'Flame' colored 'Glo-Bug,' single-egg pattern. Photo by Franklin Smith D.D.S.

graphite design. An angler will want to have extra spools for his reel which contain both floating and sink-tip lines for varying water conditions.

Three of the most consistent 'Alaskan' steelhead patterns are:
(1) Size 2 Purple or Black Egg-Sucking Leech;
(2) Black, or Brown and Black Woolly Buggers; and
(3) size 4 or 6 Flame or 'Champagne' colored Glo-Bugs.

Leader tippets are probably best at something around 1X. Use short, three and a half or four foot leaders when fishing with sink-tip lines to keep flies from rising off the bottom, or employ a nine or ten foot leader with split shot attached approximately 18" above fly when operating with a floating line. (Check regional fishing regulations for specifics regarding split shot).

There's no question about it: steelhead fishing has a certain magic about it, and those anglers able to experience it in Alaska will not be disappointed. In Alaska, it's the numbers of fish, not their size (despite the 42 pound record) that steelheading is famous for.

Should some lucky angler just happen to catch a new state record **Oncorhynchus mykiss** *saltwaterous* in the form of a 43 pounder - please write or telephone (you can call collect) explaining all about catching it

...and wher**e.**

One thing 's for certain: Steelhead are definitely, as my 'ol fishing partner Franklin 'Doc' Smith puts it,

'Trophies ...truly worth their salt."

"Everybody Wants To Race Up To
Alaska To Catch All Those Fish.
Relax. Take Your Time.
Enjoy Yourself.
Breathe A Breath or Two of Fresh Air.
After All, Like They Say,
Alaska Might Just Prove To Be...
A Trip of A Lifetime."

Mike Hershberger, 1991

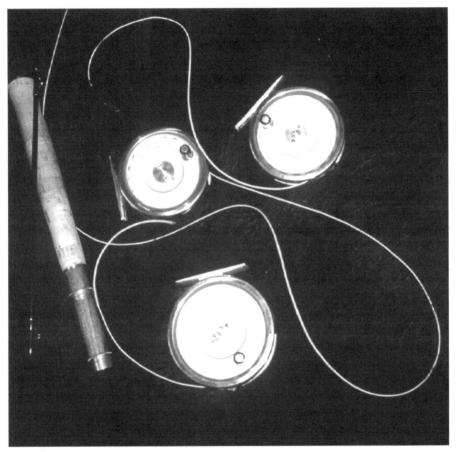

There are two schools of thought concerning fly reels for Alaska: (1) reels with drags, and (2) reels without drags. Which school you subscribe to will determine how quickly you want to land your fish.

FLY REELS
FOR ALASKA

Whether an angler prefers to crank a fly reel from the right side or from the left, (left is considered correct* for righties, and visa versa for southpaws, despite what old English tradition teaches) having enough fly reel for the fishing situation at hand can be very important. This pertains to Alaska's trophy rainbow and salmon species as much as it does to Florida's tarpon.

But, what exactly, is meant by 'having enough fly reel?'

Sometimes, selecting the 'proper' reel for your fly fishing needs isn't always what is correct for someone else. And, this pertains to Alaska, too. This may be one of the reasons why so many fly reel choices are available today. Alaska's anglers have an extremely wide array to select from, but basically speaking, all choices come down to selecting between two fly reel designs:

(1) Reels which have drag systems built in. (Disc Drags).
(2) Reels which do not have built-in drag systems. (Click Drags).

Which 'system' you choose will depend greatly upon what your perception of what a fly fishing experience should include. Do you want to make sure you 'haul' the fish in ably - or do you belong to the school that might wish to play the fish a bit longer and thus, realize the thrill of the fight a touch more?

Most of the fishing supply catalogs purport that Alaska's anglers should employ fairly large, drag-equipped reels possessing enough backing capacity for 250 yards or so of 'insurance' against such wily fish as fresh silvers, kings, sockeyes, chums, and steelhead. The fishing catalogs often suggest something like a reel having a 4-inch diameter and a stout, disc drag - enough to 'stop a horse' or something of that nature. However, there are those of us who tend to find reels like these heavy and fairly cumbersome. Personally, the last thing I want at the end of my fly rod is a big, heavy reel.

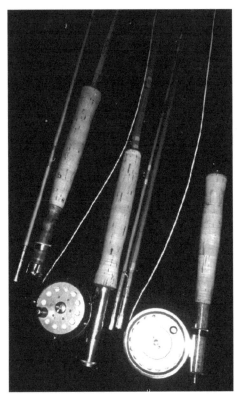

A wide variety of fly rods and reels serve in catching Alaska's fish, but the 'average' one-rod angler would do well to select something in the 8-weight category with a reel having an adequate 'drag' and sufficient backing.

The question seems to be, *Drag?...or NO Drag?*

Many anglers logically point out that having a reliable drag system on a reel only makes good sense. Most drag-equipped reels are adjustable, so an angler doesn't need to necessarily use his drag until he elects to. Others, like the late, great, extremely experienced Alaskan fly fisher, Mike Hershberger (who fished mainly with the Hardy line of beautiful, "caged," lightweight, dragless reels) always maintained that 'drag -type' reels tend to spoil the Alaska fly fishing experience. Mike argued that the angler only cheats himself by using a "mechanized winch" instead of carefully playing each fish 'to hand.' Mike Hershberger often pointed out, "People pay a lot of money and travel long distances to fish for Alaska's species - so Why should they want to finish the project in the least amount of time possible?"

Interesting point, don't you think?

For those of us who tend to believe in the No Drag theory, here's the reasoning: When a fish decides to run a bit (in heavy currents the angler may wish to high heaven he *had* purchased that disc-drag reel after all) let it! The more pressure the fish feels the more it will fight against the rod, they say. Supporters believe that a fish carefully played (even on a 'light' trout reel) will not generally leave the area or school it entered freshwater with.

The 'No Drag' believers go on to recommend the following procedure concerning the hooking and playing of fish:

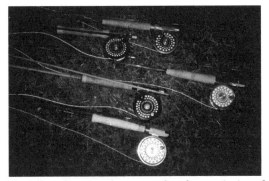

It differs from angler to angler, but majority of experienced fly fishers prefer long,, nine or nine-and-a-half foot fly rods. in most circumstances. 4-piece 'travel' rods are very popular nowadays.

94

"Lift the rod, set the hook, and then allow the fish it's freedom for a minute or two without applying too much pressure. Carefully play the fish to hand using only the rod tip and your palming hand. Then, after you release the fish (to live to fight another day for another lucky angler) that's when you'll really begin to appreciate the fishing and the feeling you enjoyed - without totally relying on a reel's drag system doing all the work for you . *Now, that's fly fishing Alaska!*"

Which school YOU choose for your Alaska fishing adventure is up to you. I tend to lean toward the No Drag Theory myself, but that could change - al-

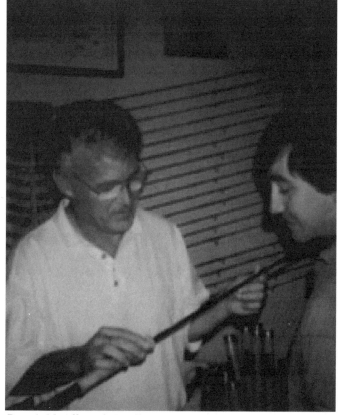

Dennis McAffee, of McAffee's Fly Shop *in Anchorage discusses new graphite rods with Alaskan angler, Brant Bunous.*

though I don't believe it will. For a beginner or newcomer I'd recommend a reel with a decent drag — just in case he *happened* to hook into a monster.

* Lee Wulff © 1989 E. P. Dutton, Publisher
THE COMPLEAT LEE WULFF
A Treasury of Lee Wulff's Greatest Angling Adventures
Chapter 2 - Pg. 12 'The Left Hand Is The Right One'

FLY RODS
FOR ALASKA

I f I had to select just one fly rod for fly fishing the 49th state, I'd be tempted to choose a 9-foot, or 9 1/2 foot 8-weight fly rod. It would be a fast-actioned, state-of-the-art graphite rod, one that wouldn't weigh much over 3.5 ounces. With it I could fish nearly every northern specie quite effectively (and have fun doing it) even though it would be too much rod for grayling - and far too little rod for king salmon.

However, an 8-weight would be close to the perfect tool for trophy rainbows, and, other than for exception-ally delicate 'presentation,' it would be fantastic as a float tube performer. It would have the power to toss big, heavy, weighted wet flies and stream-ers across wide, windy Alaska rivers and lakes, yet it would possess enough finesse to keep Dolly, char, and lake trout fish-ing somewhat interesting with-

Author's 'Hardy DeLuxe' graphite 6/7-weight fly rod and Hardy, 'Marquis-6' reel photographed next to small bear print.

out totally 'overpowering' the experience. An 8-weight would be too much rod for pinks, but barely adequate for large chums, and just about right for silvers, or fresh sockeyes (or red salmon).

As much as I tend to rave about it, I *don't* believe an 8-weight fly rod is the one, magic, fly rod for all of Alaska's fly fishing needs. I *do* think it comes closest of all fifteen choices, however. To my way of thinking, an 8-weight can be a bit on the light side for the larger salmon, as these species can tear-up an angler on either a 9-weight or even a 10-weight. On paper anyway, an 8-weight looks as if it's the perfect rod for Alaska. However, a lightweight 9-weight is probably a better all around choice as the 'standard' for a fly rod for the one-rod fisherman in Alaska.

A 9-weight is much too light for a steady diet of king salmon fly fishing. Those who are crazy enough to go for kings on a fly rod in the first place owe it to themselves (and the fish) to purchase either an 10-weight, or a 11-weight fly rod for battling with the big kings and larger salmon.

Preferably, an angler should have two or three fly rods in his possession for fly fishing Alaska. Here is what I'd probably select if I was going shopping for fly rods for Alaska:

(1) My basic trout rod would probably be a 6-weight, even though grayling and Dollies are more enjoyable on 4's and 5's. A 6-weight is light enough to keep the fishing enjoyable, but on windy days (they can get windy in Alaska) the 6-weight will 'buck the wind' far better than a 5, and it will also throw a little heavier fly.

I'd be tempted to make my mid-weight rod a 9 or 9 1/2 ft. 8-weight, but with today's super-light graphite materials, I might just opt for a 9-weight instead. Today, a state of the art graphite 9-weight fly rod can feel like one

David Angus, of Mountain View Sports Center *in Anchorage inspects a fly rod he refinished for author while veteran Bill Mauer, looks on.*

of yesterday's 7-weights. Also, a 9-weight would have a bit more 'muscle' for fighting Alaska's larger species.

I don't actively fish for king salmon with a fly rod anymore (my last king nearly did me in) but if I was serious about pursuing kings, I'd give an 11-weight a lot of serious consideration. There's something extremely functional and useful about rods in the 10/11-weight category when an angler finds himself standing out in those big, wide, rivers, especially when the winds are present. Often, these rods seem too stiff and heavy when first waggled in a department or sporting goods store, but out on the stream they really shine.

So, there they are: Those are my basic Alaska fly rod choices: a 6-weight, an 8-weight (or a better yet, a light 9-weight) and then a 10 or 11-weight with some muscle for the really big fish.

What about fishing bamboo in Alaska?

Certainly. Tonkin cane has more than it's share of merits, as well as many followers in Alaska - just as it does elsewhere; I'm one of 'em. But I'm very careful that I try to not hook into a salmon with a valuable bamboo rod; bamboo 'sets' (or warps) are hard enough to keep out as it is.

I do recall enjoy one fantastic afternoon of fishing hot silvers with a seven-foot, 6-weight cane rod, however. Come to think of it, maybe Lee Wulff really had something with his love for shorter fly rods. I was alone that day, so I don't have any witnesses, but I got into a 'pod' of silvers numbering something like a hundred, and every so often one of them would engulf my "Battle Creek Special" wet fly and go tearing down the river, causing my old Hardy Marquise-6 reel to whirr like a buzz saw while I held on for dear life. It was a 'kick' using that old, refinished Southbend cane rod that day, and exciting, too, to discover a fantastic, little-known drive-to spot where I could fish for cohos - having the place all to myself. The only

Master rod crafter Marty Karstetter, with another of his beautifully-made tonkin cane, bamboo fly rod creations. Marty often uses modified Everett E. Garrison tapers in his fly rods.

fly in the ointment was that I forgot to write down the exact date of that experience, which would have made things just sooooo much easier the following year.

Another of my cane rods is a 7 1/2 foot, 5-weight, made with a beautiful myrtlewood reel seat, a G.S. sliding cap and band, complete with Super Z ferrules. The rod was built for me by the world's best kept secret rod builder: ex-Alaskan (now Montanan) Mr. Marty Karstetter.

Built on improved Garrison tapers, Marty Karstetters' rods are not only beautiful, they perform with a trait I call, 'sneaky long.' I generally throw a Wulff Triangle Taper 4/5 with my Karstetter rod, and I'm always impressed, not only with it's finesse, but also with it's distance. And, just like the 'ol Grand Master, himself, Mr. Everett E. Garrison did, Marty even uses dark, resourcinol glues on his beautiful fly rods.

I also have an old, nicely refinished, lime-green-wrapped Granger Special (an 8 1/2 ft. 6-weight 3-piece). It's nothing special, really, not a very costly rod by any means, but it has been a lucky rod for me, and it is fun to use. It's actually a medium-actioned wet fly rod, but I often throw dries with it anyway, just for fun. I get a kick out of seeing the faces of today's modern, high-tech anglers whenever I pull it out of it's short travel tube and assemble it. I fished it on some of Alaska's premier waters for a week while fishing with John Gierach last year (you really *should* fish bamboo while fishing with Mr. Gierach, right?) and it performed admirably. As usual, it was lucky. By the way, I acquired that refinished Granger rod from a little lady named Betty, wife of Bob, of Bob's Rod and Tackle Shop in Denver, Colorado. Years ago, Betty actually worked as a rod-wrapper for Bill Phillipson.

You've never heard of Phillipson fly rods?

A while back I owned an old, Wes Jordan-made Orvis, an 8 1/2 foot 8-weight cane fly rod - weighing something around 5.25 ounces, I believe. I had some fun with it, caught some nice fish. I obtained it from Len Codella, who used to be president of Thomas & Thomas, but who now owns Heritage Rods and Tackle in Turners Falls, Mass. Unfortunately, I traded that Orvis 8-weight rod away. I made the mistake of deciding it wasn't exactly perfect (which it wasn't) but then, few rods ever are. That's the way it is sometimes with fly rods and idealists as fishermen. Sometimes we don't really learn to appreciate a good fly rod....until they're long gone.

What would I say if someone were to ask me, "What is the one, best fly rod for fly fishing Alaska?"

My first response would probably be something like, "... Whatever rod you happen to have with you the next time you get a chance to fly fish one of Alaska's best rivers!

Not very profound...until you stop and think about it for a while.

My real answer might be: You'd be better off bringing two (2) graphite fly rods: Bring a combination of something like a 6-weight, along with a 9, or 10-weight...

...and you'll do just fine, indeed. ⸻🎣

"Fly Fishing Alaska Is Not A Matter of Life and Death"

"...It's More Important Than That."
Anonymous

FLY LINES
FOR ALASKA

T he one, single piece of fly fishing equipment most often overlooked and least understood when it comes to fly fishing Alaska is a thing called THE FLY LINE. As most anglers know (but relatively few seem to fully understand) fly lines are not fly lines are not fly lines. It's like saying all airplanes are equal. They'll all (hopefully) get you where you want to go - only, some do it a whole lot faster, more comfortably, smoother, or carry a lot more payload, etc., than others do.

It's the same way with fly lines, too. They're all different and they all do some things better than other lines do.

Many anglers seem to think the main difference in fly lines today are the various colors they come in; "...Let's see, what should I use today? the Tropical Lime line or the pretty, English-made pink floater? Or, should I use that optic orange line with the dark brown 24 foot tip they call a high-density sinking tip? Anyway, what does it matter? After all, they're all about the same length, and they all do about the same job. After all, a fly line is a fly line..."

Wrong!

There's a world of difference between today's fly lines, and each fly fisherman coming to Alaska for his first junket needs to really understand the differences.

Basically, what we're talking about here are the differences of the applications between (1) the floating line, and (2) the sink-tip fly lines. To make things seem even more confusing (they're not, really, it just seems that way at first) there are different tapers of floating lines, and even more types of sink-tip lines. For practical matters, however, let's consider there are only two lines available: the floating line and the sink-tips. Now, the fisherman only needs to understand when to choose a floater and when to choose a sink-tip. Simple enough.

(1) **Floating Fly Lines**: Whenever you see one of those lovely, English-looking advertisements in the fishing magazines, the ads that show a flyrodder casting a beautifully-controlled, tight loop with a colorful fly line arching over his head using a "..such and such" fly rod, chances are the guy in the photo is casting a *floating* line. 'Floaters' are generally many times more pleasant to cast than are their sink tip counterparts. Why? Floating lines handle and cast much easier. And, since they ride high on the water, they're ever so much easier to lift.

(2) **Sink-Tip Fly Lines**: Sink-tips feature heavy, somewhat awkward, high-density, 10, 13, 20, or 24-foot sinking tips that are usually drab brown or dark gray in color. The colored portion of the line connected to the tip is called, 'the running line," or running, or 'shooting' portion of the fly line. These colored portions are often manufactured thin to 'shoot' well, or slip through a rod's guides easily. To say that a sink-tip is less pleasurable to cast than a floating line is usually considered true by most fly fishers. That is speaking broadly, however, because not all sink tips are totally unpleasant to cast. It's just that the floaters are their most enjoyable fly lines — whenever an angler can get away with using one. Confused yet?

With a floating line an angler can enjoy his casting all day long. And, a floating line permits the angler to SEE his fly line through every dent, ripple, or chop of the water's surface. A highly visible color allows him to see to mend his fly line (to straighten it) in varying or conflicting currents. A floater is generally easier to 'pick up off the water' and make a backcast with than a sink-tip. With a floating line an angler will usually want to use a longer leader - to get his fly down to the correct depth (where the fish are hoped to be). And, oh yes, it doesn't really matter much what color a floating line is because all lines (as silhouettes on the surface) appear black to any eyes watching from below. The only time an angler might be cautious with a brightly colored line would be during false casting (when the angler is casting back and forth above his head to dry the fly or change directions) or at the time of presentation. (Fish have been known to SEE fly lines zipping above them in the air, become frightened, and dart away).

Many beginners believe that employing a floating line means necessarily fishing on, or near the surface. This seemingly logical thinking isn't always true, however. A floating line stays on top of the water, true, but if it has a weighted, long leader, together with a weighted, heavy fly, this rig will serve more than adequately in getting a fly down deep, near the bottom. This process, using a floating line, is broadly called, 'Nymphing.'

With a floating line the angler can have his cake and can eat it, too. He can SEE the movements of the fly line on the surface, he can cast with complete ease, and he can still get his fly down deep or fish on, or near the surface - all depending upon what mood he's in that day.

Nymphing (a fairly modern term which means to fish a nymph, or immature, wet fly pattern) is often accomplished via a floating line. Anglers frequently place 'strike indicators' near the end of their fly lines (if they aren't opposed to adding a piece of foreign substance), attach a long leader, and sometimes a weighted fly (depending on the water depth he's fishing) and maybe a split shot or two about 18" up from the fly. Then, as the fly sinks and begins to drift, the angler watches the strike indicator for sudden movements or quirks (or any unnatural movements) and then raises the rod tip - or 'strikes,' setting the hook. Unnatural movements signal the presence of a fish - either a fish that's hooked itself, or a fish that's mouthing the fly. How the angler reacts to these movements determines his abilities as a wet fly fisherman. The art of fishing just under the surface (the damp fly technique) continued from days approximately forty or fifty years ago when silk lines would half float and half sink: usually about six to 12 inches under the surface. Thus, the 'Damp Fly Technique' often heard about in Atlantic salmon fishing.

Obviously, floating lines are used primarily for dry fly fishing, which is another way of saying the fly is supposed to float on the water's surface - and hence remain "DRY." What could be simpler than tossing a floating line with a floating fly attached to the end of a long, tapered, floating, mono leader out, across the water's surface, allowing the whole 'system' to float - and begin drifting along at a natural pace with the current until a fish comes up and gulps it? (And they say dry fly fishermen are a mighty breed)!

"HE's good! He fishes with a DRY FLY!"

In my opinion it's the WET fly fisherman who deserves all the credit. He's the one who is forced to 'fish blind.' It doesn't take many beginners long to realize that actually being able to see a fish 'flash' under the surface as it 'takes' a wet fly is a bonafide art form. "The Art of Nymphing," it's called.

"Master, when will I KNOW the fish has taken the fly?

"When the orange sun sets in the east, oh ye of little faith..."

"Oh, yeah...*sure*...I see."

One of the most common errors committed by Alaska's fly fishermen is using the wrong sink tip fly line at the right time. However, you've got to give any fisherman a certain amount of credit anytime he ascertains the need to use a sink-tip fly line in the first place.

Good Thinking. Logical. Makes Sense.

The only thing askew is ...our friendly weekend angler often has the wrong sink tip line on his spool for the water conditions that he's now facing. Try telling Mr. Average he should be carrying three sink tips, all on extra, separate, expensive spools and there's a good chance he'll look at you like you're some kind of crank!

An absolutely correct crank, but a crank ...nonetheless.

There are fishermen who come to Alaska to catch fish - and there are fishermen who come to Alaska and catch a lot of fish. Unquestionably, the biggest reason for this is not the flies these guys are using. Instead, it's their fly lines, which determine, more than anything else, which water level they'll be fishing-at after making their casts, ... and thus the amounts of fish they'll find at these depths. The key point to remember is this: fish at the correct depths for the specie/s your after. For example, Pacific salmon are usually caught *deep*.

Here's a point all of Alaska's anglers should know and remember: Pacific salmon tend to hug the STREAM BOTTOMS. They're usually found in the DEEPEST waters. Because some anglers don't understand this fully, they'll end up drifting their flies (or lures) OVER salmon all day long - never seeming to understand why the other guy is the one catching all the fish. For salmon, you've GOT to get the fly DOWN deep.

To do this a fisherman needs to understand the various densities of sinking fly lines and sink tip lines (which are merely shorter versions of the sinking lines that are already attached to the end of a fly line). Basically speaking, if you can count from one to six you've got it made. A type one sink tip line doesn't sink as quickly as a type six line does.

Each fly line manufacturer has it's own method/s of numbering their lines - and each of them are constantly coming out with improvements, some better than others. But, basically, sink tip lines are either made to sink slowly or sink fast - and in Alaska you'll want the latter kind, believe me. In most situations you'll need to get the fly down *quickly* - especially in heavy, deeper currents.

Some of the most enjoyable and productive lines for fly fishing Alaska are the Teeny series of 24 foot sink-tip fly lines. These come in T-200, T-300, and T-400 series. The "T" stands for Teeny (Jim Teeny, the designer) and the 200, 300, and 400 stand for the weight (in grains) of the sinking tip portion of the lines. A T-400 requires a stouter rod to throw it - because the sink tip portion of a T-400 weighs more than a T-200 - but the T-400 sinks faster, and also gets the fly down to the fish quicker. *Trade offs.*

In my opinion a Teeny T-200 is adequate for about 75% of Alaska's salmon, char, and rainbow fishing. I believe a Teeny T-300 (thrown by an 8-weight or 9-weight rod) is about 90% adequate - because it gets down to the fish quicker. When you get to throwing the T-400 from a 9-weight or 10-weight rod, you'll begin to lose a bit of finesse, but you will get the feeling of 100% bottom effectiveness (it gets a fly down) fast!

There are many other modern sink tip lines created by various manufacturers that an angler might want to consider for Alaska's fly fishing. The Scientific Anglers 'Steelhead Taper' Type V fly line is an excellent, quick-shooting, fast sinking, easy mending 13-foot sink tip that is terrific for the majority of Alaska's fly fishing situations. I have a grey, Type IV that is a very good line for casting and mending, if just a tad slow in the sinking department for some of Alaska's deep, swift streams. For medium, or shallow streams it's ideal, however. Cortland manufactures a fine sink-tip line in their Type 6. It comes in either a 10, 20, or 30-foot sink tip configuration, I believe. It's a fairly high density sink tip that is excellent for many fishing situations in Alaska.

Of all the sink-tip lines available (I prefer floaters and fish them whenever I can) I probably rely on the Teeny series of sink-tips most often. I probably use the T-200 over the T-300 more often because it is so wonderfully adaptable to many situations, even though it doesn't sink quite as quickly as the T-300. An angler can use a T-200 to great advantage with 6, 7, 8, and even a 9-weight rod in a pinch. A T-200 will cast long distances for large, feisty salmon and trout ...all day long without becoming overly heavy and tiring to cast. It isn't a line that will wear an angler out or cause 'fly fishing elbow' the way some lines will.

I rely on my white Teeny T-200's or my orange T-300's with their 24-foot dark brown sink-tips .... any time I can't go with a floating line, *instead.* ⎯🪶

FLIES YOU
CAN COUNT ON

I t amazes me how some fly rodders can keep up with all the hundreds of new fly patterns there are to select from nowadays. Take a closer look at any of the fly tying manuals available (Tony Route's new book, "Flies For Alaska," Johnson Publishing Co. ISBN 1-55566-087-8 appears to be excellent by the way) and you'll notice that there are literally hundreds of Alaska fly patterns for an angler to select from, and that's not even counting all the standard, old 'regular' fly patterns in existence.

But, here's what I'd like to know:

(1) How's a guy supposed to *select* one Alaska fly pattern over another ?...and,

Sculpin

(2) How in the world can a guy tie more than a few dozen patterns (enough to last him three lifetimes) and still keep his sanity?

A few years ago it finally came to my attention. It had to, there was no avoiding it any longer. My fly vests were becoming entirely too heavy and bulky. I was getting loaded down with far too many fly boxes and zip-lock freezer bags full of "killer patterns." Like many fly fishers, my pockets were literally bulging with far too many flies, gadgets, and paraphernalia.

I'm not even close to being in the same league with Alaska's *Dan Jordan* as a fly tier, but I *had* hand-tied many of those flies myself, so there was a part of me that didn't want to get too far away from any of them at any one, given time for fear a voice from heaven might catch me 'unawares' on the stream one day with words sounding something like,

"*...Try the purple Woolly Bugger with the pink palmered hackle and the* *white, fluffy tail, dummy!"*

For all I knew, I'd miss the fish of a lifetime if I didn't have the world's largest assortment of flies in my pockets so that I'd be able to pick 'just the right

fly' at 'just the right time.' And that's not counting the pounds of other junk that accumulates in a fisherman's vest - stuff that not only seemed desirable when you bought it - but also seemed totally *necessary* - at least at the time, anyway.

Looking back, I've rarely heard voices at the river (telling me which fly to use, anyway) so I've given up on trying to carry every pattern ever devised for hooking Alaska's sport fish species.

Krystal Bullets and Sparkle Shrimp

Now I only carry a few proven patterns, patterns that I know perform well. I've developed a good amount of 'faith' in my selection of Alaska fly patterns.

There are no secrets to my list - only fly patterns that have produced well for me over the years. Here they are:

•DRY FLIES•

I've yet to meet a rainbow trout that wouldn't readily inhale my favorite dry fly pattern, the **Adams Irresistible.** For my purposes it works best in a size-12 or size-10. I think the fish take it to be a drowned moth, I'm not sure. All I know is, it sure catches fish.

Its' deer hair body will float all day long (especially if I give it a 'grease'

treatment before wetting it) and fish seem to take it with reckless abandon most of the time. It looks very 'buggy' floating on the water, but fish may mistake it for a mayfly or caddis, I'm not sure. If I'm *really* serious about catching rainbows on the surface I'll use an Irresistible with an abdomen that I've marked with a dark 'Magic Marker' creating circular spirals imitating a bee. I don't know for a surety if it makes the fish strike any faster, but I BELIEVE in the Irresistible, and because of this

Royal Coachman dry fly.

it is a superb fly for surface feeders like rainbows in the evenings. 'Ya Gotta Believe!'

My one, personal dry fly favorite for Arctic Grayling in particular catches grayling at the surface like there's no tomorrow. Believe it or not, it's a size-12

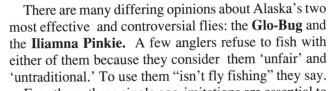

or 14 **Griffith's Gnat.** I don't know exactly what bug the fish think they're seeing when this big fly drifts past them, but it excites them like crazy - grayling in particular. It's peacock herl body (which looks very bug-like) is probably the key to success. This fly doesn't float as well as some of the other dry flies, but it's effective if fished damp, just under the surface, too. Looks like a small Woolly Worm with it's Grizzly, full-palmered hackle. One of the things I like most about this effective pattern is that even I can tie them well.

I shouldn't neglect to mention the **Black Gnat.** Grayling are famous for being associated with small, black flies - and the Black Gnat is one of the best. Will take other species regularly, too, including rainbows. Sizes 12-16.

There's no denying the effectiveness of a **Royal Wulff** or it's predecessor, the **Royal Coachman.** These brilliant, red attractor dry flies are as effective in Alaska as they are in the lower 48. Anytime an angler casts a Royal to the surface he's asking for action. Nobody seems to know exactly why these flies produce so well. My guess is the peacock herl as much as the red color. Great producers.

Elk Hair Caddis: Anglers who are hooked on these flies are really hooked. These imitations look almost identical to the real thing as they drift along with the currents. Try darker bodies when in grayling country. Deadly pattern.

Blue Dun Parachute: What dry fly fisherman's fly box is complete without a few classic dry fly patterns? What could be more fun than hooking sipping rainbows during mornings or evenings? For a real thrill try size 18's on 5 and 6-pound rainbows. Grayling like them, too, especially in size-14's or 16's.

Black Foam Ant: These new, foam-tied terrestrials are amazing producers, plus they have the added advantage of floating 'all day.' The foam used by the pro fly tiers is a special type with concentrated air cells - causing it to float forever. A couple of turns of Grizzly Hackle and your 'ant' is ready to catch big Alaska rainbows and grayling. Red foam is available, too, for those who might have an affinity for 'Red Ants.'

•WET FLIES•

NYMPHS, & STREAMERS

There are many differing opinions about Alaska's two most effective and controversial flies: the **Glo-Bug** and the **Iliamna Pinkie.** A few anglers refuse to fish with either of them because they consider them 'unfair' and 'untraditional.' To use them "isn't fly fishing" they say.

For others, these single egg-imitations are essential to any Alaska fly fisherman's box, and some anglers wouldn't go astream without them. They're Alaska's versions of

Glo-Bug

"matching the hatch." Tied in a variety of colors, including the entire 'progression' of deteriorating eggs: Flame, Orange, Pink, Peach,

107

Champagne, Red, and Black. Champagne is considered most productive color. Good for Dollies, char, lakers, rainbows, grayling, and salmon. They're routinely tied on short, O'Shaugnessy style hooks.

Egg-Sucking Leech. These purple Woolly Buggers with purple, palmered hackle and pink chenille, single-egg heads are currently Alaska's 'hottest' wet flies. Good for all species, including rainbows and silvers (which nail them hard on the swing , drift, or retrieve). My first king salmon on a fly rod (a 35 pounder) was taken on a size-4 Egg Sucking Leech. Called the, "Alaska Express Fly" by many - Don't fly fish Alaska without it. This

Egg-Sucking Leech

fly provokes sharp, hard strikes for some reason. For real fun, try it along cut banks, or bounce it along the bottom of a riffle.

Black , Brown , and Olive Woolly Buggers or Leeches: Don't leave these 'old' standards behind for newer creations. Still 'tops' as a fish catcher, a favorite Alaska wet fly. Great for steelhead and silvers. "The Electric Leech," a Bugger with iridescent flashabou tied-in, is a particular favorite of mine and many others. Big rainbows (and steelhead) attack these flies hard- especially on the 'swing.' The olive Woolly Bugger has been a

Woolly Bugger

favorite producer for years.

Pink and Purple **Popscicle:** My favorite chum fly, works well with pinks and silvers, also. Pulsating, magic maribou fibers tantalizes fish or irritates them - who knows? They work! Try stripping them through holding water, and hang on.

Hares' Ear Nymph

Hares' Ear Nymph: Produces in Alaska as well as it does anywhere. These and Woolly Worms are great twitched at surface, creeped to the surface, on the retrieve, or simply drifted or tumbled. A favorite of float tubers. Always a dependable fish catcher.

Flash Flies and Krystal Bullets: Silvers, chums, Dollies, and pinks strike these bright wet fly patterns with reckless abandon. A size-2 Flash fly is the best silver salmon fly I have ever used, with the exception of an Egg-Sucking Leech, which seems to work on just about everything. Tied weighted, these flashy attractors get down fast. The 'Fall Favorite,' a similarly tied, flashy steelhead pattern, also serves well in accomplishing many of ؛ same tasks.

Flash Fly

Polar Shrimp, Babine Special, 2-Egg Sperm Fly, and Battle Creek: These pink and orange-colored flies are some of Alaska's best patterns. Char and rainbows are highly attracted by them. Especially effective during salmon seasons or used during early season on hungry fish.

Smolt and Fry Patterns: Thunder Creek, Black Nose Dace, Blue Smolt. For springtime or early summer fishing, try tumbling these fish-imitating stimulators. For lakes, get ready for action when using sinking lines and stripping through milling fish. Imitate wounded bait fish. A sparse, purple or brown tying creates a fabulous 'blueback,' or (red) sockeye fly.

2-egg Fly

Northern Pike Patterns: The deer hair mouse or a large, gaudy, colorful marabou pattern or streamer will serve nicely for attracting a pike's attention and provoking a strike. Big, fluffy Woolly Buggers or Electric Leeches will do the trick in a pinch, too. Cast the fly over to the weeds or lilies close to shore, strip it back to you, and hang on...!

My experience has shown me the flies listed above are consistent producers. They will enable an angler to meet almost any Alaska fly fishing challenge with confidence. On the water, your fishing guide can quickly show you when and how to fish each particular pattern.

Honorable Mentions: Other excellent fly patterns that work well in Alaska and should be mentioned include:

DRY FLIES: Humpy, parachutes, blue dun, beetles, hoppers, ants.

WET FLIES/NYMPHS: Bitch Creek, Montana, Prince, Stonefly, Tellico, Zug Bug, Woolly Worm, Hares Ear Wet, Muddler Minnow.

STREAMERS: Lefty's Deceivers, Matukas, Zonkers, Mickey Finn.

ALASKA'S
BEARS

Sooner or later, whether he wants to or not, sometimes when he most expects it and often when he least expects it, the Alaska fly fisherman will come in contact with 'ol Ursus, or the Alaska Brown Bear. The main thing for him to remember is: just keep your 'cool.' Chances are, the bear he's seeing has encountered hundreds of other fishermen in the past.

You're just one of hundreds of fishermen the bear sees annually.

Alaska has it's share of black bears, too, of course, but blacks are usually shy, retiring creatures that frequently go out of their way to avoid humans and remain in cover. Never take a black bear for granted, however. During my hunting days and I learned that black bears are tenacious and can be vindictive. Actually, more humans are injured by blacks than by brownies, but that's another story...

All bears qualify as being 'unpredictable' creatures, despite how trite this description has become over the years. One never knows when a bear may continue walking in the direction of a group of anglers just to show "it owns this piece of river," or, it might just duck into the alders never to be seen again. Some brownies will pretend they don't see you, and some actually seem so myopic that they apparently DON'T - until they can smell you, at least, and only *then* are they able to determine that you're *Human,* and not just another bear.

It goes without saying to always treat every bear with respect and keep out of their way. Walk slowly to give them room, but **NEVER RUN.** Predators usually react to running by chasing, so always keep your cool and move slowly. Most bears will go to lengths to avoid human contact. Chances are the bear you've spotted has encountered humans many times in it's lifetime, but don't misconstrue that all bears consider humans as being superior creatures. Sometimes it seems just the opposite. Some bears seem to go out of their ways to demonstrate their superiority in an area (or that they are ' boss,' at least for the time being, anyway). This is usually accomplished by a bear walking slowly in an angler's direction, acting as if it hasn't yet noticed the angler/s. The game is over when the angler/s moves off and makes way - giving the larger animal the right of way.

In case someone might be considering bringing a firearm along for protection, keep in mind that individual had better be a very experienced marksman, or he's gambling with wounding a bear—a mistake that could be very costly. Bears are extremely easy to wound, and hard to kill. Consequently, you'll probably be better off allowing bears to have their right of way.

Recently, a group of four of us experienced an interesting bear encounter. Wishing to do a little dry fly fishing for rainbows and arctic grayling one morning, we were flown from King Salmon to a lovely dry fly spot at a small bay where a creek enters a large lake. From the air, as our pilot circled the area in preparation for our landing, we sighted a brown bear sow standing with her two cubs at the mouth of the very stream we wanted to fish.

"Oh, don't worry, she'll go away..." the pilot muttered as he lowered the flaps on the deHavilland Beaver and cut the throttle for our landing in the little bay.

"Just shout at her and tell her to go find another fishin' hole!" he continued. *"She'll skidaddle..."*

A few minutes later we'd offloaded our gear and were waiving good-bye to the pilot who was now revving his engine and taxiing for takeoff. Leaning his head out of the airplane he reinforced that he'd return in about four hours to pick us up and return us to the lodge. A minute later the beaver disappeared in the horizon.

Alaska's bears are curious creatures that usually have only one thing on their minds: Fishing. *Always allow bears the 'right of way,' and keep a minimum of 50-yards distance. Photo by Eberhard Brunner.*

We looked around us in silence. The brown bear sow and her two cubs were still feeding just 60 yards away.

Naturally, the next things to do were: rig our rods, assemble our gear, and kick the sow and her cubs out of *Our Fishing Hole.*

Sounds simple, right?

"Hey Bear...Hey Bear...Get Out Of Here!" "Go On, Take Your Cubs And

112

Go Find Yourself Another Place To Fish Today... This Is Our Spot....!!!...Go On...Get Out Of Here...You ... X..X..X ...!!"

We all took turns yelling at the bears at the top of our lungs.

Nothing. None of those bears budged in the slightest. Could they hear us over the sound of the rushing stream water? All the three bears did was continue to fish...paying absolutely no attention to any of our 'commands.'

The clincher came about three hours later. We could hardly believe it. One of the cubs inadvertently wandered over to the beach where we'd piled our extra gear when we first arrived. There it started sniffing around. After a minute or two the cub realized it was sniffing human scent. Suddenly, it stood up, squealed just like a brown bear cub is supposed to squeal, and started hissing.

Instantly, Mama (who had suddenly grown 100 pounds larger) and the other cub ran over to protect the 'endangered' cub. Finally, after sensing that everything was 'okay,' after frantically looking around in all directions, all three bears wheeled and hightailed it into the thick stuff and out of this true story.

Suddenly they had just vanished!

Did we humans smell *that* bad?

Apparently, over the course of four hours, the bears hadn't even realized we were humans - un*til junior had smelled us* - even though we had been stand-ing only a few yards away and were yelling at the top of our lungs.

Ted Gerken, of Iliaska Lodge, *examines brown bear prints discovered along remote, Iliamna river. Ted and his wife, Mary, are among Iliamna's fly fishing pioneers.*

It's possible that none of those bears had ever seen a human before, I can't say for sure. But, come to think of it, it WAS a fairly remote fishing location we'd been dropped-off at - more than a little off the beaten path.

Now, after a few months to ponder and look back on that situation, I'm willing to bet those bears simply took us as other bears. Maybe all those stories about bears being half-blind are true. What I *do* know, however, is that bear*s' noses don't lie*

Alaska *on the Fly*

On another occasion, on my first visit to famed Lower Talarik Creek with Frank Plunk of Big Mountain Lodge, I had a brown bear sow stand up just 40 yards from me and begin snapping her teeth just in the middle of my backcast. Instantly I felt the blood drain from my head. I knew my face had turned a pale shade of stark white. Somehow I got the sneaky suspicion the sow wasn't really in the mood for any new games just then, so I refrained from the customary small talk and banter and quickly commenced in respectfully addressing her by her official, honorary, and deserved name: "SIR."

I found myself looking down at my 3 ounce, 6-weight Sage graphite fly rod and wishing it was a .375 H&H Magnum, instead.

Later, I learned that Mama (capital M) had had three cubs with her all along (none of which I could see in the brush at the time). I had inadvertently walked right into their living room.

Typical Alaska brown bear encountered along Alaska salmon river. Never allow bears to learn that you have a fish on your line. If this happens, point your rod at the fish and pull back sharply, breaking the leader , severing your connection to the fish. Photo by Eberhard Brunner.

...all's well that ends well, as they say, but I'd learned what adrenaline tastes like that day, I guarantee.

I didn't really feel too bad when Mama and her three cubs ran across stream from me a few yards upstream and disappeared into the brush. If I remember correctly, it was just about then that a fine rainbow took my egg-pattern, helping me to 'forget' all about those bears and go on and continue my fishing...

Bears can do crazy things that sometimes don't seem to make any sense. Once, while fishing an unnamed stream in the Kukaklek area, a group of four of us spotted a blonde bear standing on it's hind legs as it gazed from about 80 yards distance. We'd just finished eating lunch, and all four of us yelled at the bear telling it to go away, and eventually it did. It dropped to all fours and ambled away, just like a good bear should.

About fifteen minutes later, however, some of us noticed 'another' blonde bear running hell bent for leather, seemingly headed for the next county - running away from us in the opposite direction. *Then* we realized it was the same bear we'd seen just minutes earlier. What had happened, we reasoned, was that 'our' bear had wandered over to where it had crossed the prevailing wind currents (which had revealed our human scent) and the bear panicked. That bear reacted by running as fast as it could, (like a Disney cartoon bear) apparently right out of the territory.

Bears depend on their noses much more than their eyes to authenticate a human encounter.

114

On another occasion, a group of three or four of us were walking from the lodge at Brooks to where the floating pontoon bridge crosses the main river. As we came to the point in the trail that makes a sharp right-hand turn, a brown bear suddenly emerged from the river just below us and climbed up to where we had been walking. Before we knew it, another bear approached from the bushes on our right. We didn't panic, but moved off quickly and methodically. You can't imagine our astonishment when, a minute later, we turned and saw the two bears begin copulating, almost as if we humans didn't exist. Slowly, we continued our walk to the bridge, where we finally stopped and stared, and rubbed our disbelieving eyes.

And I thought I'd witnessed nature in the raw before...

Each bear encounter is usually very different. A lot of it seems to depend on the mood of that particular bear that day. Fortunately, the vast majority of Alaska's man/bear encounters end up being entirely harmless. At times it seems as if both species have to 'put up' with the other species' presence. And, both species of 'animal' generally want to put distance between the other, all the while maintaining some degree of dignity in the process.

You can keep the dignity. If it's alright with you, I'll just keep my distance...

It is very important that anglers DO NOT allow bears to discover they have a fish on the line. If you see this be-

Brown bear at Brooks River Falls in July of the year. Bears disappear for a week or two during August as they go in search of berries before returning to the river again for one last look-around before winter, and hibernation ,sets in.

ginning to happen, break the fish off your line by 'snapping the line' (by pointing the rod at the fish and quickly pulling straight away) if you think a bear could possibly sense that you have a fish on. The last thing you would ever want would be a bear galloping over to check-out a new-found fishing hole...*with you standing right in the middle of it!*

What humans need to remember in bear country is:

(1) Fishermen are but visitors in the BEARS' natural environment. It's *their* backyards!

(2) Alaska's bears are primarily interested in only one thing: Fish and fishing. Bears have fish on their minds, not humans. Just don't go tiptoeing around surprising them, and everything should go just fine. Be especially careful around sows with cubs. Remember to make your share of noise while in bear country. Sing out loud if you have to, even if you might not sound exactly like Englebert Humperdink.

Remember that *fish* are what bears depend on primarily for food, and *fish* are what bears are constantly looking for, except in August when they go off for a time to pick berries before returning to the river again for one last look around before seeking hibernation for another winter. Don't kill fish and then leave them hanging around your tent or campground unless you're looking for what is classically referred to as a,"... *bad encounter of the brown kind.*"

Bears rely on their noses much more than any of their other senses. Hearing comes in a distant second place.

Always have respect for Alaska's bears and always allow them to maintain a degree of dignity. Bears are very proud animals. Try to always allow them a wide passage. There will be times that anglers will have to inform bears of their presence, either by hollering or talking, but usually the situation will dictate to the angler which tone of voice to use. Always treat bears with respect and do not mock them. Talking loudly and making plenty of noise as you travel through thick country will generally alert bears of your presence and avoid any confrontations. Some people wear tin cans on their belts with loose pebbles inside to rattle as they walk to alert bears of their presence. Be cautious not to step between a mother and her cubs, even if the cubs are large two year olds. Remain close to your fishing partners and talk loudly to avoid bear encounters. It is often said humans should keep fifty yards away from any bear and a minimum of 100 yards away from a sow with cub/s.

Alaska's anglers *will not* encounter bears on *every* Alaska river on every day of their Alaska fishing vacations. Some days simply produce more bears than others, and your guide/s will know how to handle each bear situation. Remember, most bear 'encounters' are innocent, so keep your cool and use common sense. Chances are the bear/s you're seeing have had numerous encounters with humans in the past. As far as they're concerned, you're just another one of those 'strange human beings' that doesn't represent any competition for *their* fish.

One thing is for certain: Bear encounters are always exciting, stimulating wilderness experiences. They can cause an individual to reflect on the wonders of nature in The Great Land like few other situations can. Ninety-nine times out of 100, brown bears will go out of their way to avoid an encounter when they realize humans are present.

For up-close viewing of Alaska's brown bears or for premier bear photography I suggest visitors make it a point to experience Brooks River at Katmai National Park. As this is written they're building a new bear-viewing stand at Brooks, just across the pontoon bridge from the main trail and only yards from Brooks Lodge. Contact Katmailand, Inc. in Anchorage for details on dates and accommodations at Brooks Lodge. Overflow guests can find lodging at Quinnat Landing Hotel in King Salmon (a 20-minute floatplane ride away from Brooks) when additional rooms are required. Flights to Brooks River and back are made by Katmai Air on a multi-daily basis from the Naknek River in King Salmon.

Eberhard Brunner, reknowned outdoor photographer, specializes in bear viewing and photography in Alaska's Bristol Bay region. Eberhard conducts a series of photography workshops each summer at his, "Big Bear Bay" camp for individuals wanting to expand their horizons with a camera lens. Eberhard Brunner's brown bear and wildlife photographs are easily the finest I've ever viewed. ──✸

116

ALASKA'S INNS AND HOTELS
- Rooms On The Edge-

A nyone contemplating traveling a long distance to Alaska needs to decide which type of experience he and his party is desiring. Stated bluntly, Alaska isn't Alaska, isn't Alaska. After experiencing many of The Great Land's lodges, guide services, camps, facilities, and fishing operations, I believe I'm beginning to get a fairly good idea of the variety of experiences that exist 'in the bush.'

One also begins to get a better picture of which activities might be best suited for individual types of travelers. For example, those who might be best suited for boating large rivers might not be considered perfect candidates for 'Gary's Wilderness Extravaganza,' a mere 3-day climb from sea level to the crest of 'Mt. Maxima'...located some 13,578 feet in elevation overlooking the mighty Zentina.

Visitors will want to spend a bit of time considering the alternatives before making their final decision.

Matching the client's desires to the final destination only takes but a little listening and a touch of knowledge about Alaska's alternatives. But by the way some agents go about writing their bookings you'd think every visitor actually wants to sleep in a campground tent.

When are people going to realize that Alaska has other alternatives that exist between a full-blown fishing lodge or camping out with the college kids and granola set?

Hey! What about us regular, middle aged folks?

Those better suited for a more comfortable life-style situated on the edge of the wilderness might just appreciate something more along the lines of the dining, comfort, boating, big water drift fishing, and affordable luxury they'll discover at an Inn or 'Bush Hotel.'

Whenever I think of 'middle-class visitors' who might not wish to fork-out the expenses of a full-blown lodge yet still desire to be near "the real Alaska" and still wish to retain some modicum of comfort, I think of Brooks Lodge at Katmai Park, or Quinnat Landing Hotel on the famed Naknek River at King Salmon, just a 20-minute floatplane ride from Brooks.

Lem and Anesia Batchelder's Iliamna *Airport Hotel*, located at Iliamna Airport near the Newhalen River, comes to mind, also. Lem's just finished refurbishing the place, after purchasing it from 'ol John, the previous owner. With 24 rooms upstairs (most double occupancy) with a couple of 'quads,' and a 'common' toilet facility, it's the kind of place that can begin to look like *The Ritz Carlton* of Iliamna, Alaska in a hurry - especially if its been raining or gusting outside.

Actually, Brooks Lodge at Katmai is set-up in a somewhat similar fashion, if you want to look at things that way. Brooks is a series of separate, clean, spacious, cabins (27 in number as I recall) which offer guests complete privacy, including a shower in each cabin (yes, there's plenty of hot, running water) a sink, and comfortable beds. Just a short walk down the path from the cabins is

Ouinnat Landing Hotel *in King Salmon, Alaska is located only yards from the prodigious Naknek River where great fishing can be found. Quinnat offers guest a variety of life-styles, '..from Fly-outs and Filet Mignons to drift fishing and regular old, hamburgers.'*

the "lodge building" itself, where delicious meals are served, buffet style, 3 times daily. Visitors may also enjoy the comforts of a lounging area around a warm, friendly fire. When you see it you'll know what I mean when I say; Brooks Lodge will look like the *Beverly Wilshire* after you've spent a day fishing or photographing bears.

I've overnighted at these places and others on many occasions in my fishing travels across Alaska, and I can highly recommend the values these 'Bush Inns' offer. They're not exactly lodges, but they do accomplish some of the same things lodges do. These places are, in reality: *Bush Inns and Hotels.*

They range from operations like John and Joyce Logan's, *Skwentna Road-house* (great salmon and pike country located up Susitna Valley across the inlet from Anchorage) all the way to modern, unique *Quinnat Landing Hotel* on the Naknek River in King Salmon. These places are excellent alternative accommodations for those individuals interested in visiting Alaska on a more casual, less-defined basis. They offer comfortable beds, clean sheets, and 'maid' service, if not room service. Sometimes some of the more remote "Inns" include a sink and some running (if not hot) water. In the case of Quinnat Landing, it's as comfortable as anything quality inn in 'the city,' and bush flights arrive and depart every few hours to some of Alaska's premier wilderness fishing and photographic areas.

Or, maybe you'd be happy just stepping out front of the Hotel or Inn, boarding a boat, and drift fishing for salmon for an hour or two before brunch?

For those middle-aged or older citizens who might not wish to go to the effort of pitching a tent at a campground (especially one with brown bears walking around at night) these 'Bush Hotels' become more of a necessity than anything. And, that brings up another trait of these places: visitors can often select from the type of life-styles they desire. Often, it's all there...from Filet Mignons and freshly-caught seafood...to hamburgers and french fries. You make the choice of the life-styles you're wanting. At Quinnat Landing in King Salmon, for example, on a Friday night visitors probably won't know for sure whether they're in Anchorage or King Salmon while they're busy enjoying themselves in the upstairs restaurant. On the other hand, don't forget that just outside, across the mighty Naknek River, lies the beginning of 'The Real Alaska,' the very same Alaska that rugged outdoorsmen travel to, either for photography, hunting, or Alaska's premier fly fishing.

I call these places, "Hotels on the Edge," meaning, 'on the edge of the wilderness.' They're found all over the state, but travelers usually have to search them out a little to find them. Nowadays, these places are highly sought, as opposed to being viewed as neither lodge nor campground. I like 'em and my guess is, you will, too. After all, why NOT enjoy Alaska with some degree of 'affordable luxury' if you can't afford a full-scale lodge?

What it all boils down to, in the end, is a warm shower, a dry, comfortable bed, and some degree of privacy. Maybe you'll just want to sleep-in tomorrow, who knows? Prepared meals are nice to have, too. Ladies, especially, seem to appreciate the little things, like walls for one, while spending time in 'Alaska's Bush.' Having a real door to keep 'critters' out at night will go a long way to keeping smiles present.... as opposed to the 'ol tent with the torn wind flap, and a hard, lumpy bedroll. Just having a bonafide kitchenette

John and Joyce Logan at Skwentna Roadhouse *and Fishing Lodge. Great salmon and pike fishing, comfortable accommodations, and great camaraderie. Joyce's T-Bone Steaks are among the very tastiest in Alaska.*

and warm food available is considered to be desirable, too.

Some of us simply aren't as young as we used to be.

On the other hand, I ask you, who really WANTS to sleep on the ground when they could 'rough it' during the day, and relax in 'affordable comfort' at night, with the amenities of a hot shower, a hot meal, and a warm, dry bed?

The truth of the matter is: More and more tourists are visiting Alaska each year, it appears, and that's probably a good thing. Alaska's residents can be pleased that something, at least, seems to be going in the right direction regarding Alaska's economy for the nineties. Heaven knows we'll probably never see another heyday like we had during the "Pipeline Days," and the Exxon Valdez cleanup is apparently over...and Clinton..sure isn't...

By the way, where IS Cicely, Alaska?

WEATHER PERMITTING

There's a saying in Alaska that goes, "If you don't like Alaska's weather, just wait a few minutes...and it will surely change." *Whoever said that knew what he or she was talking about.* Next time you get the chance, take a good, hard look at a topographical map of Alaska. Pay particular attention to both the mountain ranges and the coastal valleys. What you'll see will be the disparity between those areas at sea level and where some of North America's tallest, most abrupt mountains begin. It short, it gets steep...*very quickly!*

Alaska has a way of reminding humans that Mother Nature is the boss. Pro pilots know this, and amateur pilots need to always remember it. Even Alaska's brown bears sometimes hide under bushes until Alaska's winds quit gusting. And, if you've never tried casting a fly line in Alaska's winds, it'll teach you the differences between using a 4-weight and an 8-weight fly rod - *quickly.*

But it isn't *always* windy in Alaska. Sometimes it's so spectacularly calm and clear that a person can become completely addicted to the place and be caught-up in it's pristine wonders. It isn't difficult to become completely mesmerized...sometimes forgetting that Mother Nature is always watching.

Many of the trips I've made from Anchorage through Lake Clark Pass to the Iliamna area stand out in my memory. Pilots who regularly fly "The Pass" know it's an awe-inspiring site of jagged mountains and huge, weathered glaciers. Maybe it's not as treacherous as Merrill Pass or Rainy Pass, but don't try telling that to the families of the dearly departed that didn't make it. Their survivors know better.

Along the valleys of "The Pass" are wandering, ever-changing glacial streams, often chalky from the amounts of glacial silt they carry with them in their journies to the lower elevations and Lake Clark, itself. It's beautiful country, with meandering tributaries and many steep, rugged slopes.

Alaska *on the Fly*

The first time I ever flew "The Pass" I was in the backseat of Tom Bukowski's (Wild Rivers) Piper PA-12, "The Doctor's Cub" as it's called. It's a beautiful, blue and white, fabric-covered bushplane that is equipped with large, 'Tundra Tires' which allows Tom to set the airplane down almost anywhere. One of the things I like about PA-12's over Super Cub PA-18's are their wide, comfortable, rear seats which were made for two passengers. Tom's plane has also been modified with additional windows.

It's about a two and a half hour "cub" ride from Anchorage to Iliamna. Tom and I could speak through the airplane's headsets as he piloted the craft. Together, we marveled at the beauties as they passed by. The weather was perfect. Those awesome glaciers and mountain peaks seemed surreal. We experienced no problems whatsoever during the flight, not even any turbulence at the other end of the pass near Lake Clark. I remember that beautiful first flight through those picturesque mountains and glaciers as if it were out of a dream.

Yet, on another trip through 'The Pass' things were very different. I was with another pilot and we were flying in a Cessna-182, a metal-covered, fast-flying, small-wheeled, single-engined, 'city' airplane. During this trip the cloud socked-in, dark, grey, and thick, totally blocking our view of the surrounding topography.

'Soup' they call it—*Thick soup.*

That's when I remembered we were flying through some of the steepest mountains I'd ever seen in my life...

It would have been nice to turn around and head back to Anchorage ("The Pass" is wide enough in some places to make a turn) but because we *couldn't see*, the only option we had was to drop down to a very low altitude and follow the glacial river below as it snaked it's way down through the rugged valley.

I remember it as the kind of experience that reminds you that you should have gone to church more, should have been nicer to people, and that if, (PLEASE, GOD, if only you'll allow me one more chance) you'll take out the garbage and be nicer to the dog from now on...

Being an ex-paratrooper and being used to flying, I wasn't exactly scared, at least I wasn't about to puke, not just yet anyway. However, I *was* giving more than a little thought to what color of tie I wanted to wear to church that next week...

Then we hit turbulence. My head bounced off the ceiling of that airplane so hard it hurt. NOT THAT I MINDED IT MUCH. What really had me worried was NOT BEING ABLE TO SEE THE MOUNTAINS as we flew through those thick, grey clouds at something like 125 M.P.H.

By the time the terrain began to widen where we could start to see splotches of grey mountainside and a few trees here and there we began to realize there was still another treat waiting for us; Heavy winds careening off the tops of the hills from our port side...

But, we'd made it through 'The Pass' at least...

However, our fun wasn't over yet.

Actually, it hadn't even begun. Below us we could see where white caps were forming on what had been minutes earlier a calm, aqua blue Lake Clark.

Then it occurred to me for the fifth or sixth time that we were on wheels - *not floats...*

I turned and looked at my friend the pilot, my good, good friend, the pilot. He was a good, good pilot, too. I even told him so, right then and there. Why wait? I mentioned something about how cool and calm he seemed, even as I spoke!

Actually he *did* appear to be composed, although he didn't look nearly as composed as he'd looked before the winds had come up. I could tell that he was not overly pleased about losing control of the situation, however.

I wanted to tell him I wasn't exactly pleased about losing that last 150 feet of altitude either....but, from the look on his face, I decided not to open my mouth just then. I thought it might be better to let my friend the pilot concentrate on his flying ...at least for the time being, anyway.

Fortunately, we crossed Lake Clark without further incident, except for getting bounced around about a bizillion times more than we cared to be. My head hit that ceiling a couple of more times.

Then I began to notice that the path of the airplane didn't necessarily correspond with the direction we were headed. Apparently we were flying 'cockeyed' on purpose in order to compensate for a quartering wind, I'm not sure. Nevertheless, it's a strange sensation, a 'must' for those who haven't tried it.

Eventually we made what is called a 'hot,' bouncy landing at a hand-made dirt strip behind the pilot's lodge. We came to rest just feet shy of the lodge building itself, the nose of the airplane not ten feet outside the kitchen door.

Our approach to the air strip had also been a wild, quartering affair. *Landing* sideways is even more exciting than *flying* sideways, I believe. Landing sideways? I'm still trying to figure that one out. Somehow I can't get used to landing in a southerly direction while the airplane is pointing southwest. It's even more of a special treat when you're coming in at 125 m.p.h.

What we experienced that day was a 'routine' uncomfortable private airplane flight- 'routine' in that it just happens that way sometimes, whenever you get caught in Alaska's weather. There's little else to do but wait out the ride and hope everything turns out. Of course, the ideal scenario in a situation like this would be to turn around and return to point A again. But that's not always possible in "The Pass," especially in thick "Soup." When one of Alaska's storm systems moves in, man is quickly reminded he's at the mercies of the heavens, and *he's* not the boss, after all. *Mother Nature is the real boss.*

I know another guide who relates the story of getting caught in a storm up near Kotzebue in the springtime after he'd flown up to inspect his lodge following a long winter. It started snowing shortly after he arrived, and by the time the storm blew over and the snow had finished falling, fog moved in, and hung around for close to a week.

The lodge owner's single-engined airplane was on skiis, but he had to spend a couple of days digging out. By that time weather reports indicated other storm systems had moved-in between Kotzebue and Anchorage, so there was nothing for him to do but wait things out. Finally, after rewinterizing, then dewinterizing his lodge again, the weather began to lift and the lodge owner could begin his return flight home. When all was said and done, his 5-day trip to Kotzebue and back to Anchorage had turned into three weeks.

But, during summer, and fishing season, Alaska has it's share of awesome, clear, 'bluebird,' summer days. Daylight lasts nearly 24 hours, so with a little help from the midnight sun an angler can literally fish around the clock, especially if he can catch a wink of sleep now and then.

When it's clear and calm and blue in Alaska it's as pretty as any place on earth. Those glacial-covered mountains projecting up into the blue heavens are always an awe inspiring sight. Want to see a sight so scenic that it appears almost imaginary? Then take a look at the Iliamna Range from 'over the top' at around 12,000 feet on a 'severe clear' day and tell me if you've ever seen anything prettier in your life. There's Kodiak, there's St. Augustine, down there's Kamishak Bay and McNeil River. Another panorama visitors owe it to themselves to see is the Alaska Range, with Mt. McKinley and Mt. Foraker dominating the horizon looking like massive, brilliant orbs. It's a sight visitors and residents, alike, never tire of seeing.

But, it's no secret that Alaska's anglers can run into inclement weather during their stays. This generally translates into winds and rain, so it's essential to be prepared with adequate raingear, and an extra wool sweater can come in handy, too.

Last year I showed up for a September fly fishing junket at Dennis McCracken's *Copper River Lodge* at Iliamna where the weather surprised us and did a complete three-sixty. 'Indian Summer' would be how I'd describe our first two days, and then ice began forming on the river edges in the mornings, and I found myself spending half of my fishing time trying to borrow a hat (with earmuffs, please) and an adequate jacket. Ironically, this 'seasoned-Alaskan' (yours truly) ended-up talking a visitor from California (I *said* Ironically) to lend me some extra clothing. Purchasing clothing wasn't ruled out, either.

Someone had to know how to dress correctly for Alaska's fall fishing...even if it had to be a Californian. *I certainly didn't*...at least not during *that* trip, anyway.

Neoprene waders can go a long way to keeping an angler warm and dry from the chest down. On the positive side of things, some of those rainy days make for some of the best fishing.

Much of the flying done in Alaska seems surprisingly low at first, but Alaska's bush pilots prefer to keep below the clouds, keeping lakes and rivers in sight at all times, all of which aids in overall navigation. Most low level flying is done over wide tundra plains or in river valleys, with high mountain ranges being miles away in the distance.

Probably the best weather advise for Alaska's visiting anglers is: don't expect to be too rigid in keeping return schedules. Alaska's occasional inclement weather might just keep a visitor grounded for a day or two longer than he'd originally planned. For a first timer, any return delay might prove irritating, but after a second or third trip, after the angler really begins learning how to catch and release fish, bad weather will be something he sees in a whole new light.

It'll be something he'll be praying for! —

ALASKA'S BUSH AIRCRAFT

L ike many Alaskan fly fishers, I look forward to the flying required to get to Alaska's remote, wild rivers. To me, half of the fun involved in fly fishing is the flying. Okay, maybe not half - but a good portion, anyway. As far as I'm concerned, it's great adventure to skim Alaska's tundrasides and through her valleys in a small bushplane and marvel at the beauties of The Great Land's rivers and varying terrains.

Come to think of it, I don't think I know of a fly fisherman who doesn't enjoy the flying nearly as much as he does the fishing. Each trip to Alaska's bush country to experience a wild river is an integral part of another spectacular experience....*Regardless* of how many fish are caught.

Flying through Alaska's mountain passes during good weather offers spectacular views. This photo was taken from cockpit of deHavilland Beaver on way through 'Lake Clark Pass' to Iliamna's premier fishing country.

In Alaska, airplanes are probably viewed in a light very similar to what automobiles are in Los Angeles; everybody seems to have one, and you don't get around very well without one. The beauty is, flying in Alaska (when the weather cooperates) can be an exciting adventure. If you're like me, and are not a licensed pilot, there's something very romantic about prying your body into a backseat of an airplane that's about the same size as a fruit basket.

The funny thing is, you'd think the older a person gets, the easier it would become to climb in...

DeHavilland's 'Beaver' model can carry approximately five anglers, plus their gear. Beavers are among Alaska's most dependable aircraft, considered by many, 'The Cadillac of Alaska's skies.'

Alaska has very few roads, and those rivers and streams located on Alaska's road systems often become overcrowded with drive-to anglers. To get to where Alaska's *creme de 'la crem* fishing is... you usually have to fly there ...or you simply don't get there. It's as simple as that.

Flying and Alaska go hand in hand. Anchorage's Lake Hood, the busiest float plane 'port in the world, buzzes like a beehive from mid-May through September of each year, many of the floatplanes carrying anglers to wilderness rivers and lakes that would otherwise be totally inaccessible if it weren't for aircraft of one kind or another.

Ketchum's Air Service, located at the north shore of Lake Hood, is probably Alaska's largest air-carrier service, and it's difficult to visit Lake Hood and not see a Red, White, and Blue Kecthum airplane in the process of either taking-off or landing.

A close-up look at the radial engine of one of High Adventure Air's beautiful deHavilland Beavers. These multi-cylindered engines have the power to lift 5 anglers and their gear from small Alaskan lakes in very short distances.

Two of Alaska's favorite sport fishing aircraft are; the Piper 'Super Cubs' and deHavilland's 'Beaver' model, a 9-cylindered, radial engined number that some anglers refer to as, "..the Cadillac of Alaska's skies."

Beavers are big and roomy and seat five or six passengers. Super Cubs, on the other hand, can squeeze in only one, or in the case of the '47 PA-12, two passengers. The Super Cubs are the champions, hands down, of getting into and out of small places, but the Beavers also do extremely well, especially for an

126

airplane of their size.

At different times of the year you can find Alaska's bushplanes equipped with regular tires, large, balloon-like 'Tundra Tires,' 'pontoon' floats, float and wheel combinations (or amphibs) skiis, or ski and wheel combinations. Aircraft owners and lodges determine which landing gear will best meet the uses of each particular aircraft at certain times of year, and *that* gear is installed, if possible. Frequently, however, Alaska's pilots find themselves wishing they had *the other* landing option— *other than what they have presently.*

Flying and fly fishing go hand in hand because many rivers and streams are accessible only via small aircraft. And, al-

Alaska West Air's *Bell, 'Jet Ranger II' Helicopter hovering above a remote, wild Alaska river. Being dropped-off via helicopter is an ultimate Alaska fishing experience.*

though many of Alaska's tundras and river valleys often look to be accessible and easily traversed from the air, they can end up being, in reality, tangled, nearly impenetrable swamps when man attempts them on foot. Consequently, if a fisherman finds himself wanting to fish another river, 'just over there,' chances are good he's going to be *flown* over there or he simply isn't going to fish 'over there.' And, that's another thing about traveling in Alaska; distances in the north country can be much farther than they appear.

When wilderness lakes of large enough proportions are available for landings and take-offs, floatplanes can plop down almost anywhere there's adequate water depth. The pilot lands, taxis to the lake edge, and the anglers and guide/s disembark. Whether or not the pilot stays around for a while

'Tundra Tires' enable 'Cub pilots to take off and land from some of Alaska's remote, wilderness locations. Here, Tom Bukowski, of Wild Rivers, ties-down his Piper PA-12 at a secluded, remote location near one of Alaska's premier rainbow trout rivers.

and fishes depends upon how busy he might be and how good the fishing looks.

'Small, Super Cub' types are the aircraft most favored for getting in and out of tight places. But the payload is limited to only one passenger. One pilot I know boasts he can get his 'Cub off the ground and airborne in something like 47 feet, and I'm not about to doubt him. Super Cubs have extremely large wings for an airplane their size. The negative side of a 'Cub is that it can carry the pilot, and one passenger and his gear at a time.

DeHavilland Beavers, on the other hand, can haul large, heavy payloads, and can takeoff and land in nearly as short of distances as the Super Cubs. Usually, five or six passengers (depending on their size and weight) can climb into a beaver.

But deHavilland Beavers are not only expensive, they are expensive to operate and maintain. That goes in triplicate for deHavilland's

Floatplanes enable Alaska's lodges and fishermen to access lakes and rivers that are otherwise inaccessible via Alaska's few road systems. Floatplane shown is approaching for river landing on the Kvichak River near Big Mountain Lodge.

single-engined Otters, an airplane so large it makes a Beaver look like a Super Cub by comparison.

Naturally many other small aircraft are seen in Alaska's skies: Maules, Cessna's (the C-180's and C-185's and C-206's are among Alaska's most relied-on small aircraft), TaylorCrafts, Citabrias, Pipers, even a few remaining Stinsons ...you name it, not to mention a host of twin engined commuters used by some lodges for transporting clients from Anchorage to distribution points in Alaska's bush regions.

Dr. 'Joe' Chandler readies his float-equipped, Cessna-185 for a fly-out fly fishing trip from Quinnat Landing Hotel *in King Salmon, Alaska.*

Today, Alaska's skies are filled with sportsmen flying here and there and to and fro in all manner of aircraft. But the two workhorses of Alaska's skies seem to be the Piper Super Cubs, the Cessna 180's, 185's, and 206's, and the 'ol 'Cadillac" itself, the grand lady of Alaska's skies, the deHavilland Beaver.

Whenever I think of the Beaver's larger brother, the deHavilland Otter, I can't help but think about Alaska West Air's beautiful red beauty, or Craig Ketchum's fleet of deHavillands, including their beautiful, new, Turbo-powered Otter and Beaver. But the Otter that comes to my mind most often is probably Katmailand's powder blue workhorse, *'ol 491 Kilo* if I remember correctly. Anyone who's fished Brooks River much has surely formed visual images of 'ol John at the stick, chuggin' across Alaska's skies, flying that grand, baby-blue and gold workhorse from Brooks to King Salmon and back ...

... as if he could fly that old warplane blindfolded.

The deHavilland Beaver called the "Cadillac of Alaska's skies" by many is one of Alaska's most frequently used bush plane.

BUSH
CARRIERS
and AIR TAXIS

S ome of Alaska's most attractive fishing lodge packages seemingly include every little detail an angler might need to fish The Great Land in comfort. Often, anglers are met at the airport by the lodge manager in the lodge van, driven to the lodge, shown to their deluxe rooms and accommodations, and then served refreshments before climbing aboard the floatplane for a little afternoon fly fishing before dinner is served at 6:00 p.m. These lodge guests soon learn they are being treated to the 'ultimate Alaska fly fishing experience.'

That's great - for those who can afford it.

But for others, however, (those of us who might best be described as 'middle class anglers)' there *IS* a way to have our cake and eat it, too.

Flying to some of Alaska's premier locations can be less expensive than many might think, and the enjoyment of flying (when weather permits clear visibility) is always a bonus to go along with the fishing.

Katmailand's *deHavilland Otter ('ol 491 Kilo) readies for takeoff from Brooks back to King Salmon, where it will pick-up another load of visitors bound for Brooks Lodge.*

Let's say a couple of anglers arrive in Anchorage with fishing on their minds.

131

Their plan is a good one: to rent a car or motorhome and hit the road and see what develops. But, within hours they decide they really *ought* to see 'the real Alaska'...especially since they've come this far, anyway.

Now, it *would* be hard to refute their logic. The 'real' Alaska begins only about 20 minutes by airplane outside of Anchorage.

Fact: It is almost always cheaper to take a commercial airline to the town nearest your selected fishing site and then hop a local air taxi to the final destination. Use the air taxis for

This Branch River Air Service *Cessna-206 is but one of several aircraft for carrying passengers to many Alaska's remote, fly fishing locations from King Salmon.* Branch River Air *also operates three beautiful deHavilland Beaver aircraft.*

the 'pinpoint' drop-offs. This way, by taking advantage of 'jet-engined, commercial airliners' you can fly over the top of weather,' and avoid any delays during your main journey. At the halfway point you'll have the expertise of a local, air-taxi pilot (who knows the topography like the back of his hand) to take

you to your final fishing site.

However, if your trip by aircraft might be only a day trip, here are some things to keep in mind:

The key thing to remember is: ask *specifically* for what it is you're wanting and don't accept other alternatives. For example, if you were

One of Ketchum Air Service's *Standard deHavilland Beaver bushplanes. Ketchum's Air Service specializes in one-day fly-out fishing trips from Anchorage.*

to go walking into just any old air taxi and say, "Can you take us fishing?" some carriers might have you in the airplane and airborne so quickly you probably wouldn't know what was happening. It would be like walking into a used car dealership and asking, "...can I buy a car here?"

Before you knew it they would have you leveling-off at 2,500 feet, soon to be dropped-off at a some sort of 'bush' river, a river 'of their convenience,' although not necessarily a pristine river.

Once there, they'll drop you off, wave good-bye, and wish you 'good luck.' They'll promise to return at 5:30 or 6:00 to pick you up and return you to

Piper Super Cubs, like Bob Couey's shown here on large, tundra tires, can get in and out of remarkably 'tight' spots. Good for pilot and one passenger only.

home base. If you get picked-up by 8:00 consider yourself lucky.

Fair enough. But not quite specific enough.

If our two anglers had bargained for the above scenario, they'd have short changed themselves. They'd have gotten everything they asked for, *except* their Alaska dream trip, the very trip they'd wanted, their *final destination*.

Oh, sure, they'd have caught a few fish, but what specie/s? and in what condition? A few spawned-out reds might not qualify as the fantasy 'trip of a lifetime' someone had originally had in mind.

On the other hand, *IF* our two fishermen *had* requested a specific drop-off destina-

Ketchum Air Service *is understandably proud of their new Turbo-equipped deHavilland Otter which can fly at much faster speed than standard Otter. Ketchum's at Lake Hood, Anchorage, is one of state's largest, most-experienced air carriers.*

tion, they could have, (for nearly the exact same fee) enjoyed one of Alaska's pristine fly fishing destinations. The trick is knowing *where*...and pinpointing it on a map for the air service.

Why settle for hamburger if steak is going for the same price?

The trick is knowing WHERE to make that Final Destination.

How does one go about ascertaining ideas for ideal Alaska drop-off fishing sites? Here are some recommendations:

Alaska *on the Fly*

(1) Check with a professional air service and ASK for ideas from someone there having a good knowledge of Alaska's fishing areas. Realize that, the clearer you ask your questions or describe your desired fishing, the more definitive your answer will be. Ask them to recommend two or three specific fisheries based on the detailed descriptions you give. Be sure to specify the fish specie/s, you're wanting, and the specific fishing experience you are desiring -

Small stream? Large river? Lake? Float Tubing? Drifting From Boat? Camp Out? Cabin?

(2) The Alaska Department of Fish and Game can also be helpful. Be sure to list same specifics as those listed above when conversing with ADG&G representatives. Alaska

High Adventure Air Service, *of Soldotna, Alaska operates three beautiful deHavilland Beavers along with several smaller aircraft. HAA caters to both fishermen and hunters.*

Department of Fish & Game Division of Sport Fishing 333 Raspberry Road, Anchorage, Alaska 99518 Phone: (907) 344-0541

(3) Make a detailed, written list of names of fishing alternatives you learn about. Then through elimination, decided on the choice/s that will be right for you and your party. One of the most common errors made by visitors and Alaskans, alike, is rushing the outdoor experience, so don't give your trip too

little time. You can always return to the city but you may never have the chance to experience Alaska's fishing again.

Don't just hop in the first air taxi you come to, and quickly schedule a 1-day drop-off . Remember, what you'll be paying

Alaska West Air's *beautiful deHavilland Otter readies for a flight from North Kenai to 'The Real Alaska."*

for with the air-carrier will be airtime and gasoline, and it's the same distance from point A to point B and back whether or not you stay one day at point B or three. For the same, basic airfare, with a little planning, your trip can be the one you've been wanting.

REMEMBER: ASK SPECIFIC QUESTIONS AND SPEND A FEW EXTRA DOLLARS ON LONG DISTANCE PHONE CALLS.

(4) When the time comes to board your air taxi, quickly reaffirm exactly what the details of your trip will be. Where, *exactly*, will you be going? On many occasions I've had pilots assigned who'd only been informed of approximately one-half of the information they needed to satisfy my requirements. Believe me it can be very frustrating to get dropped off 5 miles from the spot you 're wanting when, just as easily, you could have been delivered to the *exact* spot.

This picturesque Alaska lake is a secret location, known only to those who've been there with Mark Bell of High Adventure Air Service, Soldotna, Alaska. The lake is so completely clear you can see lake trout cruising about, while at the lake's outlet, hundreds of trophy grayling are waiting to take your dry fly.

Don't let air taxi pilots get lazy. You are paying for a specific trip, to a specific destination, and you have the right to accept or reject any deviations from the original agreement. Situations which arise due to weather, landing conditions, aircraft type, etc., can be accepted or declined by you - as a paying client. You may wish to return with the aircraft to home base if you feel you have received a bad deal. Fortunately, 99% of Alaska's air carriers are seasoned professionals who will provide you with the services you desire. Each of the air-carriers and air-taxis listed in this book are proven professionals.

Each year I make a number of fly-out day trips from Anchorage with companions to some accessible fly fishing areas. These fly-outs are often exciting excursions that are some of our most enjoyable fishing experiences of the year, enabling us to leave the 'civilization' of Anchorage for a day now and then to experience some great, 'quick-in, quick-out' fly fishing. Over the years we've learned which air taxis offer the best service to certain areas and rivers, and which ones don't. We've learned a bit about which rivers are 'reachable' in a day's time, allowing adequate time for fishing, and then time for the return flight at the end of the day. None of us would trade these day trips for the world.

The visiting fly fisher can enjoy these same day trips.

Some of Alaska's most-experienced air services are listed on the next page.

Below are some of Alaska's most-experienced air services. Over the years I've had the pleasure of flying with each of them, and in all instances, their courtesy, punctuality, services, and safety measures have been above reproach. Each of the following Alaska bush carriers come highly recommended:

Katmai Air Service - based at Like Hood, Anchorage
and King Salmon, Alaska
Service to Katmai, Brooks, Kulik, & Grosvenor
and Fly-outs to Bristol Bay Region
Contact: Sonny Peterson, Owner
4700 Aircraft Drive, Anchorage, Ak 99502
Phone: (907) 243-5448

High Adventure Air Charter - based at Soldotna, Alaska
Contact: Sandy, Mark, or Greg Bell, Owners
P.O. Box 486, Soldotna, Alaska 99669
Phone: (907) 262-5237

Ketchum Air Service - Based at Lake Hood, Anchorage
Contact: Graig Ketchum, Owner
P.O. Box 190588, Anchorage, Alaska 99519
Phone: (907) 243-5525

Alaska West Air Charter - Based at North Kenai, Alaska
Fixed Wing & Helicopter Charters
Contact: Doug & Danny Brewer, Owners
P.O. Box 8553
Nikiski, Alaska 99635
Phone: (907) 776-5147

Branch River Air Service - Van Hartley, Owner
Flying Out of King Salmon, Alaska
Contact: 4540 Edinburgh Drive
Anchorage, Alaska 99515
Phone: (907) 248-3539

Iliamna Air Taxi, Inc. - based at Iliamna, Alaska
Contact: Tim & Nancy La Porte, Owners
P.O. Box 109, Iliamna, Alaska 99606
Phone: (907) 571-1248

Talkeetna Air Taxi - based at Talkeetna, Alaska
Contact: David Lee, Owner
P.O. Box 73
Talkeetna, Alaska 99676
Phone: (907) 733-2218

Rust's Flying Service - based at Lake Hood, Anchorage
        Contact: Hank Rust, Owner
        P.O. Box 190325
        Anchorage, Alaska 99519
        Phone: (907) 243-1595

Jay Hawk Charters, Inc. - Merrill Field, Anchorage
        Contact: George Barrett, Co-Owner
        1842 Merrill Field Drive
        Anchorage, Alaska 99501
        Phone: (907) 276-4404

40-Mile Air Service - based at Tok, Alaska
        Contact: Charlie Warbalow, owner
        P.O. Box 539
        Tok, Alaska 99780
        Phone: (907) 883-5191

Island Air Service - Kodiak Island, Alaska
        Service to: Kodiak, Afognak, & Raspberry
        Municipal Airport, Kodiak, Alaska
        Phone: (907) 486-6196

Lake Clark Air, Inc.- based at Merrill Field, Anchorage
        and Port Allsworth, Lake Clark
        Contact: Reservation Desk
        2425 Merrill Field, Anchorage, Alaska 99501
        Phone: (907) 278-2054

Regal Air • based at North Shore, Lake Hood, Anchorage
        Contact: Craig Elg, Owner
        P.O. Box 190702, Anchorage, Alaska 99519
        Phone: (907) 243-8535

Warbelow's Air Ventures, Inc. - based at Fairbanks, Alaska
        Contact: Art Warbelow
        P.O. Box 60649, Fairbanks, Alaska 99706
        Phone: (907) 474-0518

Pen Air • based at Anchorage Airport, Alaska
        Personalized Charter Service, Statewide
        Shuttle to: King Salmon, Alaska
        4851 Aircraft Drive, Anchorage, Alaska 99502
        Phone: (907) 243-2485

WET
FLY
FISHING

Wet fly fishing can be described as fly fishing's simplest technique or it's most difficult, depending upon how technical an angler wants to get or how he wants to look at things. That might not sound like a very clear statement at first, but experienced fly fishers will know that fishing a sophisticated, weighted, specialty nymph is broadly classified as 'wet fly fishing' just as much as a kid who tosses a home-made fly that sinks below the surface is also 'wet fly fishing.'

Since Alaska's five species of Pacific salmon (kings, chums, silvers, sockeyes, and pinks) are NOT especially known as surface feeders (salmon are not in the rivers to feed) fly fishermen *must* go down after them, often right down to the stream bottoms; hence, *wet fly fishing*. But salmon DO strike at flies out of habit (thank heavens) or out of irritation, or reflex - call it what you like.

The technique most commonly employed for hooking Alaska's salmon species is called, 'simple nymphing.' Simple especially if the angler understands it's concepts.

For those who don't, or who might be a bit rusty, here's a review:

Suppose you're the fly fisherman and you've just come to a beautiful, panoramic spot where a pristine, crystal-clear lake empties to form a pristine Alaskan river. Those who've been to the Brooks River at Katmai where it empties out of Brooks Lake will have a perfect mental picture of such water.

Where the currents from the lake restrict, forming a 'tongue' as they converge, you are able to determine that salmon are holding between the fast and slower moving currents. These areas between fast and slower moving water are called, "seams." If you look closely, the dark, silhouetted images of salmon can be observed shimmering against the clear, ripples and currents. But even if you couldn't see them, you'd be correct in guessing that salmon are found resting in these places. Seams and moderate-moving water are always excellent places to find holding, upmigrating fish (including steelhead) resting from their strenuous upstream journies to the places of their origins.

Congratulations. You've just identified two types of water where fish are commonly found. Not many fly fishermen are regularly able to point out these spots.

So, now you've located the fish. That's half of the battle. It's always nice to have school of resting fish spotted, ready to receive your 'presentations.' The other method (blind fishing) offers it's own rewards, but c a degree of certainty isn't one of them.

But, how do you fish for these salmon? Wet or dry? By now you've learned enough to know you will want to employ the *wet fly or nymphing* method. Why? Fishing a dry fly would only tire you out and waste time. After countless hours of drifting flies over salmon's backs you'd only become frustrated. Oh, there are some who tell of hooking silvers with dry flies, but salmon aren't in freshwater to feed, but rather to migrate to their spawning grounds. Salmon are not usually going to expend extra energy by coming up to the surface for a dry fly.

Consequently you don't waste time drifting flies on the surface many feet above resting salmon.

You *could* go with a high-density sink-tip line (a 24 foot Teeny T-300 would do nicely in this situation) or, you *could* fish with a floating line and a longer, weighted fly and leader, getting the fly down by using the 'Nymphing' method. Since a floating line is ever so much more pleasant to cast for extended periods, and you've determined the water is only moderately deep, you choose to go with the floating line, electing to use a long leader with a split shot attached.

Quietly, you make an improvised seat out of a fallen log and change spools. You thread-on the floating line with a long, nine or ten foot leader. Remember, you're wanting the fly to get down deep, and not 'bubble up' again, so maybe you'll attach a split shot or two approximately 18 inches up from the fly. Maybe, just for added measure, you'll go with a weighted fly pattern, also. This system should be entirely sufficient in keeping the fly down near the bottom - right where you want it to be ...to catch fish.

When the line is installed you can tie on the fly of your choice. This is where your instincts will come into play.

You may want to go with one of several flies, but I'd probably recommend a Glo-Bug about this time, and with complete confidence I might add. I'd fish this fly as a 'searcher,' for, if a *Glo-Bug* doesn't evoke strikes in this kind of situation, I'd be hard pressed to say what fly *would*. Salmon 'nip at natural single eggs and single egg patterns almost as frequently as any other specie.

Now you're ready to fish. Wisely, for your approach, you plan to cast quartering upstream, from the opposite side of the river, to get the fly to sink and drift right into the mouths of the holding salmon. Of course, the fish are looking upstream and you've approached from slightly behind. The water is a bit faster and a touch deeper here than you first imagined (about 4 feet it appears). Carefully, you negotiate your footing and soon you are in place, ready to begin.

About now it becomes obvious that with a weighted leader it's not going to be necessary to make a careful presentation of your fly. In fact, any 'ol flip that gets the egg-pattern to where it can have time to sink so it can drift into the salmons' field of vision will be entirely acceptable.

So, that's just what you do. You find yourself casting with a slower, more opened loop than usual. Maybe it won't be the prettiest cast ever made in the history of fly fishing, but a 'flip cast' will work all the same. By this time your fly is sinking and will soon be bouncing directly into the snouts of a school of several mature salmon, each of which will weigh somewhere around eight and ten pounds, fish much larger than the brookies you were used to catching as a kid.

It occurs to you that maybe you'd better remove the slack from your line in case a fish does decide to 'take.' You find yourself watching the end of your fly line (the joint where the line ends and the tapered leader begins - where experienced nymphers attach 'strike indicators') so you can see any sudden motion or twitches that might occur.

Carefully, you follow the fly with your rod tip, mending the running portion of your line when needs be, allowing the deeply sunken fly to continue to bounce as it hesitates here and there in the currents. At the surface, a trailing loop of fly line floats downstream from you as it hangs out from the bottom of your rod hand. Intensely, you keep the rod tip pointed at the fly as it continues it's drift.

Suddenly there's a tautness, a tightening of your line. Your rod tip begins to dip, once, then again.

Before you know it there's no longer a drifting loop of fly line, but a whirling fly reel spool that is suddenly whining at the top of its lungs.

About 50 feet out, across stream, and seemingly frozen in mid-air, your eyes catch a glimpse of a long, slender sockeye salmon with a somewhat rosey body and a slightly greenish head. From it's mouth extends a long, sloping leader that leads directly to you.

It's your fish...you did it! You've hooked your first salmon!

But the battle is far from over and you can hardly believe (let alone attempt to describe the feeling) how hard a sockeye fights!
Never in your wildest dreams did you know a fish could tear at your wrist muscles like this...never mind the scuffed knuckles you've suffered from the whirling reel handle...

Somehow, heaven only knows how many minutes later, you find yourself bringing the fish to hand, working the tired salmon into the cool shallows near your feet. There, the salmon feels gravel on its' belly, giving it yet new strength to dart away again.

You wrist is throbbing with pain...

About this time you sense you're finally beginning to win the battle. There, you can see the fish.... suddenly... then...with a lift of the rod tip... the fish is in your hands.

The exhausted sockeye's gills are working frantically as it struggles to regain oxygen. The fish looks as if it's at least an eight pounder - bigger *by far* than any fish you've ever caught before on a fly rod...!

Carefully, you cradle the fish while removing the hook. The size and length of the salmon's teeth surprise you, and you're careful not to scrape your fingers. Before you realize it you've loosened your grasp and you watch as the sockeye -*your sockeye*- swims away, back to the currents you hooked it in.

Hopefully you'll remember this day and your first salmon — *just* like it really happened, for the rest of your life. About this time it dawns on you that you don't know whether to congratulate yourself more for catching the fish on a fly rod or doing it without any coaching.

And all you know for sure is that you hope to heaven you'll be able to experience this same feeling at least another couple of hundred times in your lifetime.

DRY FLY FISHING

One look at the crystal-clear Alaska river told us we were about to experience some of the premier fly fishing of our lives. Scattered here and there across the river's surface were the tell-tale rings where rainbows and grayling had been as they'd risen to sip at drifting insects.

'Probably caddis flies,' I thought to myself, not being exactly sure what the bugs I was seeing were. Carefully, I waded out to where I stood waist deep in the translucent water, being careful not to disturb things too much.

A glance upstream told me that my fishing partner, John Gierach, had also become intently aware of the hatch occurring around him. He wasn't making a sound, but it wasn't hard to tell that he was pleased to be standing exactly where he was at that very moment, especially with a bamboo fly rod in his hand.

Slowly, I waded out a little deeper to where the water became 'waist deep.' The water felt cool on my hips where the sun had been shining. Methodically, I began stripping out enough fly line to begin casting.

Across stream, a large rainbow showed himself. I stopped all movement and watched closely for a minute or two. Now and then I could see that big fish as it rose and sipped insects. It was easy to see this particular fish was larger than any of the others I had spotted. Every few moments the big rainbow's head would emerge for an instant or two before disappearing again.

Suddenly I found myself wanting to hook that big rainbow trout on a dry fly in the worst way.

There we were - standing in water fit to drink - prettier trout water than any dry fly river I'd ever fished before in my life.

By the time I worked my fly line out in a series of false casts I spotted the big rainbow again. Fifty feet upstream and quartering away I could see where it left large, concentric rings on the river's surface where it had fed.

This glimpse had told me the 'bow would go somewhere around five or six pounds; not huge by Alaska's standards, but certainly a respectable rainbow, anyway. As far as I was concerned, it was a fish from which *dreams are made...*

Slowly I worked-out the lime-green floating fly line in a controlled loop, being careful not to make a cast directly over the unsuspecting fish, thereby possibly spooking it. If my cast was to be off in any direction I wanted it to be short,.... not long!

I thought to myself, '...wouldn't it be nice if I could hook that beautiful spotted rainbow on my very first cast...'

We were standing smack-dab in the middle of rainbow trout heaven and we knew it. Perfect dry-fly water! Absolutely perfect.

John and I were both making our first visit to John and Linda Ortman's *Wood River Lodge*, located in Alaska's famed Wood River/Tikchik Lakes region. Earlier that day we'd met-up with John Ortman, Jr. at the Naknek River in King Salmon. There we'd hitched a ride with J.J. to the Tikchik Lakes region in the lodge's Cessna-185. The flight from King Salmon across Kvichak Bay and the Nushagak River to those beautiful Tikchik Lakes nestled in their picturesque mountain range was truly spectacular. The weather was superb, and from the floatplane during our trip we saw numerous big game animals including caribou, moose, and a beautiful blonde brown bear sow and her two blonde cubs.

I picked-up my fly line and made another cast. The river was deceptively deep, flowing at a steady, smooth rate, my guess being something around 2 to 3 knots. Just a few yards away was the lodge building, itself, and it wouldn't be but a couple of more hours and Linda and the girls would be ringing the dinner bell for the evening meal.

Grayling rises also dimpled much of the river's surface around us. A glance upstream told me Mr. Gierach was still enjoying himself. Carefully, I lifted my fly line and made another cast in a quartering, upstream direction, as near as I could to where I judged the big rainbow might be. On the surface, my fly line began to 'snake' as it drifted in loose, open coils. I made what is referred to as a 'flip mend' to insure that the belly, or the 'running line' portion of the fly line didn't cause the size-12 Adams Irresistible dry fly to 'drag' in the current in any unnatural way. As any fly fisher can tell you, 'drag' is the surest way there is of 'putting a fish off' a fly.

As my dry fly continued it's downstream float I noticed more grayling beginning to surface. Many of them looked to be larger than 20 inches, and 20 inches is considered to be a trophy grayling in Alaska. Many of these grayling looked to easily approach that size.

But it was easily the numbers of red-sided rainbows I could see here and there that caused me to get excited. I was using my old, green-wrapped, Granger Special 6-weight bamboo fly rod that day, a rod that has been very lucky for me.

I knew I should have been keeping my eyes riveted on the drifting fly, but the ghost-like forms of Dolly Varden char lying near the bottom of the stream began competing for my attention. The more I squinted and strained to see them, the more Dollies I began to see. Dollies and arctic char have a way of hovering near stream bottoms appearing like mere phantoms, looking ever so much like indistinct, wiggly shadows. They make me question my own eyesight at times, even though I should know better by now.

I picked up my fly and made yet another cast. Suddenly, in a gulp, my dry fly disappeared. Suddenly, my fly line tightened, becoming suspended before me like a tightrope in the air. At it's end was the perfect picture of a 'frozen,' 24-inch, crimson-sided rainbow trout .....shimmering as it hung there in the air!

Water sprayed from the 'frozen' rainbow, high above that river's surface. It looked for all the world like an oil painting I'd seen somewhere. Then, slowly, the rainbow began a cartwheeling, backward plunge back into the river's currents.

I could hardly believe it, but I had actually hooked that big, spotted rainbow - *the very fish I had wanted to catch!*

Hurriedly, I scrambled to strip-in enough line so as to appear as a fisherman who was maintaining some degree of control over the situation. Too many yards of fly line drifted downstream from me as I hurried to "get the fish on the reel." When I did, I quickly began cranking fly line back on the spool as fast as I could. But soon it was the fish at the end of my line that started taking-up the remaining slack in my line.

Then, almost before I knew it the flashy rainbow began "going ballistic" on me, skyrocketing up through the water's surface again and again, some of the jumps appearing to be three or four feet above the water's surface.

I remember standing there, stripping line, trying for all the world to look like the kind of cool, experienced fly fisherman who had the situation under complete control, one who experiences this kind of Alaska fishing action routinely.

But complete control was far from what I was experiencing, believe me, and by this time the rainbow was feeling more like a fresh sockeye, or 'blueback' salmon than it was any 'ordinary' trout. I did my best to appear to maintain some degree of composure, but Alaska's trophy rainbows have a way of making 'novices' out of all fishermen at times.

By this time John had worked his way down nearer to my position. I could see he had a grin on his face as he watched in silence as I played that rainbow at the surface. I found myself not wanting to lose this rainbow as much as I wanted to land it.

By this time my worn, old, Hardy fly reel was singing at the top of its lungs as the rainbow quickly finished stripping the last yards of fly line from my reel. I tried applying more pressure by 'palming' the reel's outer diameter, but the added tension only seemed to put the rainbow into overdrive, as fly line backing began to burn my fingers.

A short time later the rainbow began 'sulking,' or holding deep. I found myself astonished that the 4X leader tippet I was using had continued to hold together without snapping...

How, I'm not sure, but somehow all of the sections of the old, Granger bamboo fly rod remained 'aligned.' All I could do was to hope that those old, loose ferrules on the rod stayed together so the fly line could run 'true' through the guides. Meanwhile the rainbow continued to feel like a fresh from the sea, power-packed salmon at the end of my line...

Alaska *on the Fly*

It was pure excitement standing there in that lovely river battling that trophy rainbow. Every sense in my body was on 'red alert' not to strain too hard and lose that fish.

Presently the big trout skyrocketed again, this jump looking for all the world as strong and as high as the first. I remember blinking my eyes in disbelief, stealing a glimpse at John, and resetting my grip on the cork handle. I dug-in my feet to steady myself for round two.

Ever so slowly, I managed to gain line on the fish, working it in closer, but remaining worried that my leader tippet would part at any moment. I was watchful of the rainbow's every movement.

Somehow, gradually, I managed to ease the rainbow to my waiting grasp. Gently, I clasp it by the tail, being careful to keep the beautiful, spotted creature breathing in the currents while it regained its strength. I was astonished at it's translucent, almost iridescent blueish-green color and pinkish-red stripe. It's back was topped with a proliferation of dark, dense black spots distributed across a jungle-green background.

Gently, I worked the beauty back and forth in the cool shallows, speeding oxygen through it's gills. When I could see the rainbow was strong and ready for release, I pointed it in the direction of the deeper water, loosened my grasp, and watched as the spotted beauty swam away, leaving me completely satisfied and very much at peace with the world.

John and I looked at each other and began to laugh. That fish had represented perfectly what rainbow trout dry fly fishing in Alaska is all about. A few days earlier I 'd watched John do nearly the exact same thing on another of Alaska's premier rivers, also using a dry fly.

Although this rainbow was far from the largest I've ever caught in Alaska, to this day it still remains as the *one* fish that stands out in my memory whenever I think of fly fishing for rainbows in The Great Land. In my mind I can still see that spotted beauty shimmering there in the air - *as if painted on canvas* - high above that glassy Tikchik river. —⚓

ALASKA'S FISHING LODGES

Once, a couple of years ago when I was making my first visit to one of Alaska's well-known fishing lodges, I got to know a gentleman sitting across from me who was making his eighth visit to the place. The visitor said he was perfectly pleased with the place, pleased with the food, pleased with the service. He mentioned that he was satisfied with the fishing, too. He should have been: he and his wife and brother had been traveling to Alaska from New Hampshire each year for eight years straight just to experience this lodge and it's fishing.

I was half tempted to ask him if he'd ever considered trying another lodge, just to see if he might enjoy the flavor there, too, but I decided against opening my mouth. Such a comment might have implied that the visitor might possibly be missing out on something by staying where he was, and believe me, he wasn't. I've experienced enough of Alaska's lodges to know better.

What I did, instead, was reinforce to the guest that he had, indeed, made the right choice, and that his group was truly enjoying Alaska's crem de 'la crem. Another glance at the chalkboard hanging over the kitchen listing "Today's River Choices," reminded me that I needn't have said a word. The rivers listed were among the very best in all of Alaska. The prime rib and king crab dinner we'd just finished eating also told the story well.

It's always nice to know you're experiencing the Real Alaska ...

But, then, each Alaska fishing lodge smacks of it's own flavor. That's a given. Part of it has to do with the physical geography of the place and the type of 'water' found there, and, too, naturally, part of the flavor comes from the personalities of the staff and the accommodations.

Yet, sometimes there are 'peculiarities' about lodges, too. Some Alaska fishing lodges are extremely protective about "their" rivers. Overprotective might be a better way of saying it. It's been postulated that some lodges form agreements with other lodges to create 'time shares' on certain rivers, while yet other lodges are simply *not* welcome...period, exclamation, paragraph.

I've heard about a couple of lodges that supposedly "share" a particular river. Supposedly, they divide the 7 days of the week so that lodge #1 doesn't fish on Tuesdays or Thursdays and get in the way of lodge #2. Since Sunday is often a travel day, it might also be a neutral day, a 'day of rest' for the river. Supposedly, there's also a lodge #3 that works-in a day here and there when clients warrant, but such 'schedulings' are by appointment only and only by approval of lodges #1 and #2. There's supposedly a lodge #4 that still keeps trying to become part of the 'inner circle,' but isn't getting very far.

Apparently, some of these arrangements have been standing for several years, although they're always unofficial, with nothing in writing. Hierarchy (or pecking order) at a river seems to stem from the length of time a lodge has been in operation in that area as much as anything else. New lodges are usually simply out of luck, left out in the cold. After all, the older lodges argue,

Copper River Lodge *is the epitome of 'the rustic, Alaska fly fishing lodge.' Fortunately, this wonderful lodge is also located on one of Alaska's premier fly fishing rivers.*

"Our river can only tolerate so much use - and that's that!"

Like I say, all of this is pure conjecture—pure speculation. But either way, it shouldn't affect fishing clients in any way. Either they'll get to enjoy the fruits of a well-maintained river or they'll fish somewhere else and never even know what they're missing.

After all, who could blame some 'older' lodges for feeling like they've earned some rights to certain rivers?

Looking at things in perspective, there *are* some positive aspects about rivers having professional "groundskeepers," if that's really the case. For one thing, the very presence of a professional lodge maintaining a river limits the numbers of users and protects against overfishing and killing of fish. This might not sound exactly like, "Public Invited," (and, in fact, the public, at least unofficially, is *not* invited) but this is probably to the river's benefit in many cases. Some of Alaska's premier rivers are simply too 'fragile' to handle hordes of visitors without becoming 'overburdened.' Even big rivers (the Kenai is an excellent example) can become overstressed with too many human bodies present at any one given time.

Litter is a thing anglers just don't encounter very often in Alaska, especially at the heartland's premier rivers, lakes, and streams. In the first place there aren't many convenience stores around, and secondly, the fly fisherman with enough dough to afford a quality trip to Alaska seems to be a sophisticated enough angler to know better. Most visitors wouldn't even think of spoiling a riverbank in The Great Land. Chances are extremely good that even if someone *was* stupid enough to try littering, the presiding lodge owner or manager would have that *ex-client* chastised, castrated, showered, shaved, and boarded on a return flight back to wherever he came from so fast it'd make his head swim. Other states might tolerate trash and litter along their rivers, but NOT ALASKA. During a typical day astream all shore lunches are carefully folded, boxed, or resacked, and returned to the floatplane or boat for proper disposal later that day back at the lodge.

Even though trash along Alaska's rivers isn't usually a problem, the biggest catastrophe involved in dealing with large numbers of people would be the trashing of *fish*.

Granted, it might not be an intentional trashing, but it would be a trashing of fish, none the less. Regardless of what anybody might try to argue, the sad truth is: too many average sportsmen out there simply aren't fully satisfied unless they can draw blood and kill each and every fish they catch.

Ted and Mary Gerken's, Iliaska Lodge, at Lake Iliamna, qualifies as one of Alaska's ultimate fly fishing lodges.

"Yeah! A Dead, Bloody Fish! Now, That's A Trophy!"

When are the harvesters ever going to learn that we can't go killing fish and then catch them all over again. That kind of mentality always reminds me of a famous Iliamna river that was at once time, not too many years ago, one of Alaska's premier rainbow trout streams. Now this river features good char fishing, but the rainbows? They're all but, *Adios Amigos*. The culprits? Some idiots with nets, of course. Wouldn't you know it. Can you believe it? True story, folks!

That reminds me of another strange thing about fishing lodges: Some of them have a way of changing on you... just when you thought you were starting to get a feel for the place. I'll not soon forget the first optimum Iliamna rainbow lodge I ever visited.

I remember sensing a touch of stress existing at the place, but nothing excessive, so I didn't really put two and two together at the time. I thought maybe the lodge manager was having a tif with his wife or the cook had threatened to quit or something, but I don't think the other guests ever noticed anything really unusual happening. Nevertheless, when the next year rolled around, all of a

149

sudden....*Gonzo!* The lodge was closed. Not just closed for a week or two... but closed for *Good.*

Kaput.

Seems the lodge owner in Portland or somewhere hadn't booked enough clients over the previous couple of years, at least not enough to make ends meet. About that same time the lodge manager had called informing the owner that gasoline prices for aviation fuel has a way of increasing in cost, especially when it's purchased 300 miles away from Anchorage.

Pity. It had been a heck of a fishing lodge. Really quite nice. There front room offered a pristine view of the great Lake Iliamna. Fortunately, the ex-manager quickly got another job as the new manager of another fine Alaska fishing lodge in that area, and the guides and pilots got snatched-up quickly, too.

Now, one of the original fishing lodge owners at that part of Iliamna, the next door neighbor with the blue roof, gets more of the fishing business than ever.

And, it makes sense. That lodge owner, Ted Gerken, of *Iliaska,* was one of the Alaska pioneers who, along with competitor Ray Loesche, *started* the fishing lodge business in the Iliamna area originally. Now it appears that Ted and Mary Gerken have been doing something right all along, because their business has increased

Iliamna, Alaska features many of Alaska's optimum fly-out lodges and services. Tim and Nancy LaPorte's, 'Iliamna Air Taxi' air service is located at Iliamna air terminal.

over the years, while some of their neighbors have fallen by the wayside.

Recently, I enjoyed five days of fishing with Ted Gerken and his staff at *Iliaska.* Ted saw to it that each day we flew out to one of Alaska's finest streams. After experiencing it, it's not difficult to tell why Ted's operation has remained strong over the years: *Iliaska* easily ranks among the truly great Alaska fly fishing lodges. To really experience *Iliaska,* however, visitors must ask owner, Ted Gerken to perform his infamous rendition of Robert Service's,' 'Dangerous Dan McGrew' some evening after dinner. It's Alaskan entertainment at its finest, trust me. It's better, many think, than much of the entertainment found in that cultural center they call Anchorage, Alaska.

Another excellent lodge that was forced to close it's doors in the past couple of years was wonderful *White Mountain Lodge* on the fabulous Fish River near Nome, Alaska.

White Mountain, Alaska, is a native village situated just a few miles upstream of where the Fish River empties into The Bering Sea, along the coast approximately 80 miles east of Nome. It's also an official rest-stop along the famous Iditarod Trail Sled Dog Race.

The thing that's so unfortunate about White Mountain's closing (I hear guide Paul Lincoln and others are still guiding up there for those who MUST experience The Fish River, regardless) is that it was such a wonderful, clean, modern facility and operation. And, the Fish River is a wonderful river that simply 'reeks' of north country flavor.

What killed things at White Mountain? Some say the absence of rainbow trout (rainbows are found only in the southern third of Alaska) was the culprit as much as anything else. Apparently, even well-heeled fly fishers opted for lodges situated in more southerly directions, where rainbows could be found, rather than travel all that way for only silvers, chums, char, grayling, and trophy pike.

It's not just a pity that White Mountain Lodge had to close it's doors - it's a crying shame. Mark Johnson and his crew of wonderful guides had continued the endeavors originally begun by lodge founders a decade earlier - that of creating a unique, north-country lodge that

Visitors enjoying dinner at Bobby DeVito's, 'Branch River Lodge' on the Alagnak River. Visitors won't go hungry at any of Alaska's top fishing lodges.

was bursting with the aroma (figurative) of one of the finest rivers in Alaska. Dad and I spent a week there a few years back and both of us still consider that experience one of our very finest.

Out west in Alaska's Wood River/Tikchik Lakes region, famed *Wood River Lodge* also serves as a prime example of a textbook Alaska fly fishing destination. Interested in fly fishing for rainbows, char, and Dollies in numbers sufficient enough to wet the appetites of even the most calloused, most experienced of North America's fly fishers? I still find myself dreaming about the week John Gierach and I spent at John Ortman's marvelous Wood River Lodge and the dry fly river that flows in that part of Alaska. Fabulous comes close to being an adequate description, but doesn't quite describe the area.

Another prime example of a unique Alaska flavor I really enjoy is wonderful, *'Copper River Lodge,'* situated at the southern shore of Lake Iliamna. If you haven't fished the remarkable Copper River, you simply haven't fished one of Alaska's very best rainbow streams. By the way, the rainbow trout I'm displaying on page 66 of this book is an 8-pounder caught and released on the river that flows in front of *Copper River Lodge* at Iliamna.

But the list of Alaska's impressive fishing lodges extends for many pages. To anyone considering a lodge for the first time, the choices might appear to be seemingly endless. It would be easy to recommend at least a dozen or three of Alaska's fishing lodges for one reason or another (some of them for many reasons) but it wouldn't be fair to list Brooks or Kulik Lodge, or Dennis McCracken's Copper River Lodge at Iliamna without mentioning Jerry Pippen's *Rainbow Bay Resort* or Frank Plunk's *Big Mountain Lodge* in the same sentence. The fact remains that Alaska is virtually loaded with great lodges, many of which can be highly recommended, and some that I wouldn't send my sister in law to...

It's all a matter of 'flavors,' and Alaska has 3100 of 'em.

"So, how does a would-be-visitor go about selecting a lodge?"

After the fishing and before dinner it's always great to relax and chat with other guests and talk about the day's successes.

Good question. Not a simple one to answer, but here goes:

(1) Decide on the fish specie/s you want most. This will help determine not only what time of year you'll make your visit but also which area of Alaska that is correct for you. Stated simply, you just won't find rainbow trout fishing in Nome, Alaska regardless of how badly you'd like to visit that lovely, historic town. By the same token, if it's Arctic Grayling and char fishing you're after...

You get the point. Suffice it to say you probably won't take all fourteen of Alaska's freshwater sportfish species during first visit to Alaska...

(2) Understand that all lodges specialize in some type/s of fishing and some specie/s, no matter what someone might tell you to the contrary. For example, I know of a fine lodge located on the Kenai River that is a great salmon lodge through and through, regardless of how many times they might try to explain that they're also a top rainbow lodge. They aren't, and there's a world of difference.

(3) If it's salmon fishing you're seeking, any number of Alaska's lodges can satisfy your whims and fancies. Just be sure to understand the timetables for the varying arrivals of Alaska's five species of pacific salmon annually.

(4) Talk to prospective lodges and ASK for SPECIFIC names of past guests for referrals. Then, CALL these referrals and speak with individuals that have experienced said lodge/s personally. Ask SPECIFIC questions like: "Do they have running, palatable water, and hot showers" etc. Remember, NO question is too foolish when it comes to considering a major investment in time, comfort, and travel. You'll want the lodge you choose to be so accommodating that you'll have to return again next year, no matter what the little lady might say..

It would be convenient for all concerned if someone experienced could come out and simply name a dozen or two of Alaska's best lodges and cover the matter entirely, but there are simply too many good lodge choices for that. Conversely, what becomes more important is to make sure a visitor's choice of Alaska lodge is not a poor one; asking questions like size of river/s, clarity of river/s, and available species present at an area only makes good sense.

Here's a way a potential visitor could guarantee ascertaining the Alaska lodge that best meets his needs:

(A) Decide your budget limitations and how many individuals will accompany you on your Alaska trip.

(B) Determine what fish specie/s you'll want to pursue most.

(C) Call two or three appropriate Alaska fishing lodges and ask for information regarding the best areas in the state for said specie/s.

(D) By process of elimination, determine which lodge referrals and areas are mentioned most often. Then, according to your budget, determine which lodge or lodges best meet your needs by considering fishing, services, and personalities you've talked with. Just one word of caution, however: Remember that Alaska has an almost infinite number of 'flavors' -each having it's pluses and it's minuses. Since you'll be spending a fair amount of dough, it's important that the fishing, the food, and the housing conditions, etc., are just 'what the doctor ordered.'

Please see the section at the rear of this book entitled "For Additional Information" for selecting the Alaska fishing lodge that's right for your personal requirements.

Even rainbows like this may be taken in the lakes and rivers along Alaska's road system if anglers will take the time to ask questions and explore.

ALASKA
ON A BUDGET

Many would-be Alaska anglers are discovering there *is* a way they can experience many of The Great Land's exceptional lakes and rivers - *without* the sometimes hefty price tags often associated with fly-in fishing lodges.

Nobody needs to tell you how great the fishing in Alaska is, right? Yet, all too often, 'average' anglers end up deciding something like, "..Gee, the fishing looks great, ...sure wish I could afford to do that some day."

Before he knows it our 'average sportsman' has all but talked himself out of his trip, all but totally given up on making the effort of Alaska. Maybe the IRS has come calling or maybe the kids need new shoes. Pretty soon the "average sportsman" gets to feeling a bit on the conservative side...

But, little does the would-be-angler know that:

(1) Many Alaska lodges are creating shorter, more affordable, three and four day trial packages.

(2) Fly Fishing via Alaska's road systems can deliver some good, quality fishing - even by Alaska's standards.

Still, it's difficult to educate those who think of Alaska as an exotic location that it's really just an airplane ticket away. Today, many anglers still believe fly fishing Alaska is simply too expensive for the 'average' American's budget.

Is there a way a guy can "have his cake and eat it, too?" Are any of Alaska's top quality fisheries actually within driving distance from Anchorage and located on Alaska's road systems?

Yes, and Yes.

As an Alaskan who's done his share of exploring in The Great Land, I'll let you in on a little secret. Many of Alaska's great fishing opportunities are available to roadside anglers - *if* the individual is willing to go to the trouble required in finding them. Many roadside anglers have learned that, given a little time to travel and explore, much or Alaska's best fly fishing (from Arctic Grayling to king salmon) is available to the roadside angler.

Southcentral Alaska is probably much more civilized than many first imagine. Motels, restaurants, gas stations, grocery stores and even shopping malls exist along the way. And a myriad of opportunities (motor home rentals, auto rentals, fly shops, and sporting goods stores) exist for roadside fly fishers.

So, how does one go about seeking-out these 'optimum' fishing spots if visiting Alaska for the first time?

(1) Realize Alaska is probably more civilized than many first imagine. It's not all igloos and dog sleds like some might think.

(2) Give your adventure enough time. The old saying, "...it takes either time or money" is still true when it comes to fishing Alaska's road systems. Those wishing to save a nickel must devote enough time to maximize the experience.

(3) Obtain two or three "bibles" for quick reference for traveling and fishing in Alaska. "The Highway Angler" by my friend, Gunnar Pedersen (*Alaska Viking Press*) is an excellent addition and companion reference for newcomers fishing Alaska's road systems. "*Flyfishing* Alaska" (Johnson Books ISBN 1-55566-042-8) by Anthony J. Route is another "required reading" all Alaska fly fishers should own and read. Both of these fine books are readily available at drug and sporting goods stores in Anchorage, Fairbanks, Soldotna, and Kenai, etc. Another good book for fishing from Alaska's road systems is, "The Angler's Guide to Alaska" by Evan and Margaret Swensen (*Falcon Press*). Be sure to check-out the excellent chapter on flies for Alaska in Evan's book. It goes without saying that by this time you'll have purchased your Alaska Fishing License for the length of your stay.

(4) Ask questions along the way. Alaskans are generally friendly people who are used to visitors arriving each summer. Much of the best "local info" can come from residents who are happy to temporarily share some of their favorite fishing spots with newcomers. Their knowledge of salmon runs, fishing techniques, etc., will likely surprise you.

(5) Don't travel too quickly. Stop at small communities along the way and ask locals about fly fishing possibilities. Much of your enjoyment from the trip will come with meeting many of Alaska's characters found along the journey.

Three highways lead out of Anchorage: One extends to the south (to Kenai Peninsula) and two extend north. Although there are many excellent fishing opportunities to the north, I'm half tempted to suggest the southern route for Alaska's newcomers. Why? For one thing, the southern destinations are usually easier to locate, and a little more clearly defined. Many of the northern prime spots are reached only after busting brush and exercising a bit of effort in hiking, or knowing exact locations and how to get to them.

What's the best time of year to explore Alaska's road systems with a fly rod in hand? The answer to that largely depends on which specie/s you'll be seeking: When one stops to consider that all of Alaska's fishing is heavily influenced by the annual salmon runs, having a good, basic understanding of Alaska's five species of Pacific Salmon becomes important. For example, sockeyes (or red) salmon arrive on the Kenai Peninsula about the 4th of July of each year. During odd years, Humpbacks, or Pink salmon arrive in much larger numbers than they do on even years - towards the end of July or the first week of August. Those wanting to fish for king salmon will do best in late June and into early July while the midnight sun burns almost twenty-four hours. Silver salmon fishing begins in August but often doesn't really get 'hot' until late September.

You get the idea...

Like fishing anywhere, much of the fun comes with exploring and learning "new" areas. New to first timers, at least.

Given a little time, a reasonable amount of effort, and a little luck with the timing, and there's a better than good chance that those anglers wishing to explore Alaska's fishing spots via the road systems will experience excellent fly fishing.

It may not be exactly like fishing Alaska's Bristol Bay/Iliamna, Western, or Wood River/Tikchik Lakes areas, but it sure will beat most of what fishing remains in the "lower 48" these days.

Spending a couple of weeks fly fishing Alaska's road systems can turn into a very enjoyable holiday. You'll be amazed at the fishing 'secrets' you'll discover. Some will be small, isolated spots, while at others you might be surprised at the numbers of other anglers - but either way, your's should be a good experience. Those 'average' fly fishers who might have previously thought of Alaska as being only for travelers with fat wallets will quickly learn otherwise.

Take your time and enjoy the drives and the scenery along the way. Respect private property, employ catch and release tactics on Alaska's rainbows, char, and grayling, and take a camera along with you to record 'the moment.' Don't worry that you won't be able to enjoy fresh filets along the way as you release fish. You'll get more than your share of fresh, juicy salmon, believe me.

But, be careful. Fishing Alaska via it's road systems can become addictive. My 'ol fishin' buddy, Mark Thunnel, doesn't find a way of boarding an airliner and showing up at my doorstep in Anchorage during August of each year for nothing.

"My Wife Said If I Go Fishing One More Time She's Going To Leave Me." I Want Her To Know I'm Really Going To Miss Her.

Anonymous

TAKING PHOTOS OF YOUR TRIP

During my years as Field Editor and Managing Editor of *Alaska Outdoors* magazine and *Alaska Outdoor Times* newspaper I learned to be fairly adept with a camera. Okay, maybe I'm not exactly an Eberhard Brunner with a camera lens, but I have taken a good photo here and there. I've even taken three of four photos that were deemed good enough to be front covers for magazines. Here are some of the things I've learned about minimizing the pains of obtaining decent photos:

(1) Use a small, modern, automatic camera with auto-focus that will store out of sight in a handy, easy-to-get to pocket. The smaller the camera, the better - as long as lens quality isn't effected. Why? You'll only want your camera as a tool when you're ready to reach for it. You don't need a large, cumbersome camera distracting your fishing.

Lately I've relied on an Olympus *Stylus* camera (about the size of a small fly box). In years past, I depended greatly on the performance of the Olympus XA-II series cameras (I carried two of 'em) which didn't offer auto-focus, but did provide compactness and superb lenses. Today I carry both, (actually I leave the XA in a carry bag back at the boat or airplane). I use the XA-II as a back-up.

(2) Shoot COLOR SLIDE film. I think you'll quickly begin to appreciate slide film. Why color slides instead of prints? For one thing, they're more versatile than prints, and it's cheaper to shoot slides. Another reason is: clear, detailed prints can easily be produced from a color slide, with NO loss of picture quality since transparencies are, in reality, color NEGATIVES. Also, of course, color slides can be projected, whereas color prints are limited to collecting finger prints. Color slide film can be processed very quickly (using E-6 process film it takes about an hour) and very inexpensively.

(3) Take TWO or THREE shots of each desired photo to help in coming up with a good picture. It's amazing how many 'gremlins" (like telephone wires,

gasoline cans, weird facial expressions -remember how many photos capture 'closed eyes'- or garbage and junk in the background) can creep into a viewfinder and spoil a photo. Taking two or three shots from different angles will greatly assist in eliminating resultant clutter from photos.

Be careful to handle fish gently and keep them immersed in water if you find yourself fidgeting with your camera. When you are ready, ask your subject to lift the fish just above the water's surface and you can quickly 'fire' two or three pictures. Remember to talk to the subject and attempt to capture slightly varying positions or angles.

(4) Use FILL-FLASH on all photos - even during the bright of midday -or at least on close-ups. Why? On cloudy days flash will dramatically brighten the subject. On sunny days, flash will brighten dark, shadowed areas (peoples faces hidden under hats for example). Some cameras can be switched to a position denoted as, "Fill Flash" which will cause the camera to flash regardless of external light conditions: ALWAYS USE FILL FLASH if you want better pictures!

(5) Unless you have a telephoto, or Zoom lens, shoot much closer to your subject/s than you ever before thought necessary. How many times have you received photos back from the developer only to find little tiny bodies waiving in the distance, with facial features and details so indistinct that they're barely discernible? What you're really wanting to do is shoot pictures that will clearly show off the scales of the fish, right? To do this move in CLOSER than you ever imagined necessary and capture the details of the subject holding a fish with just a touch of background. Most likely you'll be very pleased with your results.

(6) Shoot 200, 400, or 100 ASA film speeds *only*. Although many excellent speed films (such as 64, and 25 for example) are available, most compact cameras are DX -Coded to work in compatibility with full F-Stop ASA speeds. Many of today's compact cameras are not manufactured to work well using film speeds found between these stops. Therefore, don't use ASA 64 when your camera will be underexposing it because it will read it at 100. The last thing you'll want is dark grey photos from a fishing trip of a lifetime in Alaska. I often suggest the use of 200 speed film since it still retains good detail and yet, as a medium-speed film, it captures more light on many of Alaska's cloudy days. I've landed two or three magazine covers using 200 speed film, and magazine editors are constantly looking for clarity and details. Today's 400-speed films are excellent, also, so don't hesitate to use them unless you're specifically shooting for a front cover for publication. The average fly fisherman will probably fall in love with 400-speed color-slide film, and the difference in details isn't readily obvious to the untrained eye.

If you'll look closely at any of today's angling publications, you'll likely see many pictures showing a pair of human hands as they open to release a fish. This is a wonderful way to show the details of a trophy, and one which I'll be using more and more in the future.

Photographers and processors have a saying which remains as true today as when it was first stated regarding photographs:

"....Garbage in ..... garbage out!"

CATCH, THEN RELEASE

I well remember the day I wandered around a bend of one of my favorite drive-to rivers only to glimpse a huge, black dog running right at me, it's mouth open, growling, it's teeth ready to ...In the same instant I glimpsed the dog's owner, a young, plump man in overalls, standing just yards away, off to my right. He was "busy fishing" - pretending he hadn't seen me, and also pretending he was "unaware" that his dog was in the final stages of attacking me...

Fortunately the dog's bark was worse than its bite, and I didn't need to exercise my savage "elbow defense technique." But it wasn't the dog I was really upset with - it was the plump, slothful owner. It didn't take a rocket scientist to ascertain the man's feelings:

(1) This was "His" river.
(2) I was an unwanted intruder.
(3) How dare I carry a 'fishin' pole' anywhere near
his private hole?

Luckily, about this time my fishing partner fished his way around the bend. Apparently the dog owner felt that was an appropriate time to begin calling off his dog.

"Here, Killer....Here, Killer..."

I began to get the sneaky suspicion the dog owner was a bonafide slob. An angler, granted - but a slob angler, nonetheless. Like I say, it was just a hunch.

Another thing I quickly noticed was that the dog's owner carried a large revolver in a holster at his side. I guessed the piece to be at least a .44 Magnum, but probably something larger, possibly a .475 custom if my guess was right. It looked to have a barrel of approximately sixteen inches!

".. maybe I'd better not attempt to reason with this guy about the proper etiquette concerning dog ownership right now" I decided. After all, I HAD accidentally come around a corner and walked right into his *Personal Fishin' Hole!*

It dawned on me about then that the dog owner was, more than anything else, an angler with a giant insecurity complex. After all, he WAS fishing 400 yards inside confirmed BROWN BEAR country. To his way of thinking, wearing a .475 magnum revolver at his side and bringing *Killer* along for additional protection (regardless if the dog attacked humans or not) could be construed as nothing more or less than practical Brown Bear Insurance and logical, common sense.

There's no two ways about it, the dog owner was loaded for bear.

Just step outside the front porch of Dennis McCracken's Copper River Lodge *and you're ready to go fishing on one of Alaska's finest rainbow trout and salmon streams.*

Sensing that maybe we'd NOT get to fish that particular hole this day, after all, my friend and I waded up and around the dog owner (and his huge dog that was still busy barking) and found ourselves some other spots on the river to fish.

No big deal. Each of us caught a fish or two and we both had a good time.

About two hours later my companion and I turned around and began working our way back downstream.

When came around the bend, the dog owner (and his dog) was still there, still busy fishin' the very same hole. However, there *were* a few additions: The dog owner had been successful in his dredging efforts. Relying on his gooey salmon eggs he'd caught himself a mess of fish. He'd been using a big, heavy, metal spoon - with gobs of salmon eggs smeared on the hook - a temptation too attractive, I suspect, for even the most timid of fish to resist.

One of the fish he'd killed looked to be a 25-inch rainbow trout - a real beauty, a fish which looked to be about a five pounder. Along side the rainbow lay four or five chunky (but just as dead) Dolly Varden char.

The dog owner really made a killing that day.

I was tempted to walk up to him and share a few of my observations concerning the killing of rainbows with him, but my better senses convinced me that, just maybe, discretion *was* the better part of valor that afternoon. After all, those dead fish were already gone: DEAD. Chances were my feelings regarding killing Alaska's non-salmon species couldn't have resurrected those dead fish.

In my mind I can still see that bloody 25-inch rainbow and those fat Dollies lying there dead on the rocks and that smug look on the guy's face. What was he thinking if he didn't kill those fish?

That he'd starve to death?

I just don't get it; when are people ever going to learn? For a minute or two I wondered how many of those Dollies I'd caught and released from that same hole on earlier trips..

When are some people ever going to learn that we can't enjoy catching fish a second time after we've already killed them DEAD the first. Not only that, now there are no fish left to make hundreds of more fish. Let's see...One...plus one....equals four hundred!

Actually, it's a much prettier sight to watch rainbows swim away, *believe me,* I know. I've exercised both options in my lifetime. By releasing rainbows an angler can visit the same stream tomorrow if he wants .... and catch rainbows again, ...*tomorrow.*

If every angler who fishes Alaska each year were to kill just four or five rainbows each season - can you imagine how many thousands of rainbow trout that would mean had been wasted? Let alone their multiplied offspring...

Heaven, please help me to understand.

Thank goodness Alaska's lodge owners refrain from the killing of rainbow trout and most of the other non-salmon species. Thank goodness somebody realizes that Alaska IS NOT a never-ending, bottomless source of fish. Let us not forget why half of Alaska's anglers are fishing The Great Land today rather than fishing their own back yards in the 'lower 48":

They've killed all their fish back home!

"Let's see, now..oh, yes, ...it says here I can HARVEST three rainbows as long as they're all over 20 inches in length..."

Whack 'em, Harry!

When in the world are our educated state agency gentlemen ever going to think of anything other than the term that seems to be near and dear to them, the term they use frequently, the term that was devised to do the impossible: that is, satisfy all segments of society at once...

That term is spelled, "H-A-R-V-E-S-T," and 'To harvest' means to kill. In the opinions of many, too many fish and game officers spend far too much of their valuable time reinforcing the art of *harvesting.*

I ask you, ladies and gentlemen of the jury, how can we catch rainbow trout today that were HARVESTED yesterday?" I can't figure that one out, can you?

When are we ever going to learn?

When is someone 'on the Board' ever going to have the gumption to promote the idea of a stronger statewide catch and release rainbow trout fishery? After all, what's going to happen if we can't legally go killing rainbows anymore?

Is some human being really going to starve to death?

Can you imagine the size of Alaska's rainbow trout in a few years if the entire state turned to 'catch and release?' Naturally, there'll be those who'll say that after time 'a natural balance' would occur, and many of the bigger 'bows would die-off, anyway. Good heavens, if that were something to really worry about, why in heavens name is Brooks River a total catch and release rainbow fishery and why are so many of the 'bows there so big and so healthy?

Can you imagine the numbers of anglers from the lower-48 that would travel to Alaska then...just to catch and release rainbows ranging from ten to twenty pounds? And, what about those rainbows that grow to be forty-two pounds, like the current state record fish.

Explain *that* one to me if you will.

Looking back, now, I'd like to thank that angler and his dog. His example might have been just we fishermen need to think about now and then to insure that we don't go killing Alaska's heavily-spotted rainbow trout.

Ironically, releasing Alaska's trophy sport fish offers nearly as big a thrill as hooking and landing them does. Here an angler gets one last glimpse of what might be a 'fish of a lifetime.'

HOW TO RELEASE FISH

Have you ever wondered why so many fly fishermen walk around wearing forceps or 'hemostats' clamped to their front pockets of their fishing vests? The reason is for easy hook removal. Quickly grasp the shank of the fish hook (being careful not to grasp the fish too firmly with the other hand) press down, away from the barb slightly, and then back-out the hook. Before you release the fish, however, make sure it has revived and is taking-in water through it's gills at an even rate. Be sure to treat the fish gently, giving it plenty of time to regain its strength after being landed.

Listen to what experienced fly fisherman, Randall Kaufmann, co-owner of 'Kaufmann's' fly fishing stores in Seattle, Washington explains about, "How To Best Land and Release Fish." I don't think anyone has ever said it better:

"Do not release a tired fish until it has completely recovered. Firmly hold a played-out fish by the tail with one hand and GENTLY SUPPORT the fish from underneath just behind the head with your other hand. Face the fish upstream in an upright position in fairly calm water, but where there is enough oxygen to allow the fish to breathe easily. By moving the fish back and forth in this position the gills will begin pumping life giving oxygen into its system, while at the same time allowing the fish to rest and regain strength lost during the battle. Fish being revived in this manner will often attempt to escape BEFORE they are completely recovered. A good rule of thumb is not to let the fish swim away the first time it attempts to. When fish are released prematurely they will often swim out of sight, lose their equilibrium, turn onto their side and die. It doesn't hurt to revive fish longer than you feel is necessary. This will insure a complete recovery without complications. This process usually takes a minute or two, but fish that are extremely tired can require several minutes. This is especially true preceding, during, and after spawning periods. When you do release a fish, do so in calm water, allowing the fish to swim into the currents at its leisure.

After releasing a fish, move slowly, for sudden movement may spook them prematurely. NEVER TOSS FISH back into the water. If you wish to take a photo, "set-up" everything before you remove the fish from the water. Cradle the fish and lift it just a little above the water so if it should happen to fall, it will not crash onto the hard shoreline. Fish can also be laid on wet grass for a couple of seconds. Do not put undo strain on the fish by lifting it high or in an unnatural position. NEVER PUT YOUR FINGERS IN THEIR GILLS for this is like puncturing a lung. NEVER SQUEEZE fish as vital organs are easily damaged. Fish will seldom struggle when handled gently. A quick, harmless way to measure fish is to tape of measurements on your rod or buy a "fish tape" which adheres to your rod. Simply slide the rod alongside the fish in the water and you get an accurate measurement. Spring scales are deadly on fish and should only be used for hoisting a net with the fish inside. It is easy to estimate the weight by the length and condition of the fish. The important consideration is to release fish quickly and unharmed. A fish which is bleeding slightly will probably survive just fine. Even a fish that is bleeding profusely can usually be revived if you are patient enough.

Try to land fish in a reasonable amount of time. The longer some fish are played the more lactic acid builds up in the bloodstream and the more difficult it becomes to revive such fish. Most fatal damage occurs to fish through improper handling, not during the actual hooking and playing of fish. It is best not to handle or remove fish from the water. When a fish is removed from the water it begins to suffocate immediately and the risk is great that it will flop about on the bank, slip from your grasp, or that you may unknowingly injure it or literally squeeze it to death. If you MUST handle fish, be certain your hands are wet, for wet hands will not destroy the protective mucous film on fish, especially trout.

To remove the hook, gently grip the fish by the tail or jaw with one hand, removing the hook with the other. If you are wading, both hands can be freed by slipping the rod into your waders. If a fish is hooked really deep the hook can often be removed with the aid of a long-nosed pliers or forceps. If not, it is best to cut the leader, leaving the fly in the fish. Nature supplies a built-in mechanism which will dissolve the hook in a matter of days. Oftentimes a friend can lend a hand in unhooking and reviving tired fish.

A barbless hook will help insure safe handling and facilitate a quick release. You seldom have to touch the fish as barbless hooks can usually be backed out very quickly using only one hand. Under specific conditions, a net, if used properly, can be a tremendous advantage, allowing you to quickly land and release fish. A net can alleviate fish flopping and thrashing over rocks in shallow water and can greatly aid you in landing a fish when you are waist deep in water. Be careful fish do not become entangled in the net."

By using barbless hooks, an angler actually increases his percentages of landed fish. Right? or Wrong?

Right!

Believe it or not, by using barbless hooks the hook is able to penetrate deeper thus insuring a higher percentage of 'caught' fish. Try pushing both a barbed, and barbless hook into a piece of cardboard and see for yourself which hook penetrates most easily and deepest. Also, the barbless hook is much more pleasant to remove when the angler inadvertently hooks himself.

Always keep a small pair of long-nosed pliers in your vest pocket so you can pinch-down barbs on those flies you may own that are not already barbless. A good set of forceps will accomplish the same task.

Becoming proficient in "catch and release' will add greatly to your overall fly fishing experience.

COMBINATION
LODGES

T he one thing all of Alaska's visitors are searching for is a fishing lodge that offers ALL of Alaska's fish species during a one-week stay. The last thing a visitor wants is to get stuck out in Timbuktuu, Alaska, at a lodge offering only mediocre pike fishing with an occasional lake trout on the side, right? Some visitors may be seeking this kind of 'solitary refinement,' but for the majority of visitors it's, "give us all you've got in spades....and right away, please...(after all, we're paying for this aren't we)...and we've only got three more days before we have to catch the airplane to get back to 'civilization...'"

Enter the ultimate, All-Alaska Combination Lodge. Some of these lodges subtly claim to feature ALL fourteen of Alaska's sport fish species (even if they DON'T come right out and say it) along with everything else the angler needs, including generous amounts of hot, running water, and, of course, delicious appetizers and hors d'oeuvres before each gourmet dinner. *Liquid refreshments* are complimentary, of course.

What these places often imply in their advertisements is: Professional, Modern Lodge, Full Service, with fishing for kings, silvers, sockeye salmon, rainbow trout, arctic grayling, Dolly Varden, and arctic char. What they don't tell readers is what is expected to be known and understood:

And, ALL of Alaska's sport fish species ARE available at these lodges - IN SEASON!

During my travels in The Greatland there have been many occasions when I've met anglers visiting from various parts of 'the lower 48' and other countries. Without exception, when pressed a little, I've yet to meet an angler who hasn't admitted that the fishing in Alaska is great - but not necessarily quite as great as the visitor's imagination had led him to believe it would be. In our minds we tend to imagine trophy rainbows on every cast in every river or lake we come to. In reality, Alaska's fishing is far superior to that found in many places in the 'lower 48' states, but it's still fishing, and as one pro fishing guide I know *puts it, "...that's why th*ey call it fishing."

Because many newcomers have been led to believe it will be easier than it is, they somehow begin to imagine collecting ALL of Alaska's fou*rteen sport fish species during one* trip. "A Trip Of A Lifetime" it's called.

However, Alaska's visitors simply won't experience ALL of Alaska's sport fish species durin*g a one week trip* - no matter how badly they may want to. Sorry to ruin y*our day, but, look* at it in the positive: Now you have a solid reason to return for a second visit.

It's highly impossible that an angler could nab a steelhead, an arctic char, a northern pike, a cutthroat trout, a king salmon, a silver salmon, an arctic grayling, a chum salmon, a pink, or humpback salmon, a Dolly Varden 'trout,' a rainbow trout, a lake trout, a sheefish, or a sockeye (red) salmon all during one trip.

It's so improbable, mind you, that I'll wager my favorite fly rod and your choice of a new, in the box, Hardy Fly Reel to anyone who can actually accomplish such a feat during a 7-day Alaska fly fishing venture. They call catching all 5 of Alaska's pacific salmon in one day difficult - or a Grand Slam on Salmon. If that's the case, such a feat with all fourteen of Alaska's fresh water sport fish species would have to be called ALASKA's SUPER SLAM, or something of that nature. Believe me, someone would have accomplished it by now if it were possible. Nobody's even come close. In the first place, Alaska's geography is against it, in the second, the salmon runs can span 5 months.

An angler would really have to hustle to catch a sheefish and a steelhead in the same day, let alone a dozen other species in between. Sometimes it's not a just a matter of miles between a pike and a cutthroat that matters. It can be more like a matter of hundreds of miles of distance involved.

What does all this mean to the average fly fisherman?: don't come to Alaska expecting to be able to catch all fourteen sport fish species during one trip. If you can experience four or five of Alaska's species during your stay, consider your trip a blazing success.

Some of Alaska's great Combo Lodges DO come close, however. One is *The Great Alaska Fish Camp*, located at Sterling, Alaska where the Moose River flows into the aqua-blue waters of the Kenai.

Of course, other great Combo Lodge choices exist: Katmailand's Kulik, Grosvenor, and Brooks Lodges - all within a hop and a jump of one another in the middle of Alaska's heartland, an area called "Angler's Paradise." Bobby DeVito's Branch River Lodge on the Alagnak, is another, and John and Linda Ortman's Wood River Lodge in The Tikchik Lakes region of southwest Alaska is one of the best combination lodges I can think of.

As you've probably discerned by now, it's really the sockeye salmon that are responsible for much of Alaska's great combo fishing. Combo Lodges found in the 'Bristol Bay' area, in Western Alaska, and near Lake Iliamna are deluged with thousands upon thousands of sockeyes which initiate the fishing action annually. Myriads of 'reds' entering fresh water to begin spawning 'turn the wheels' of yet another season of sport fishing in Alaska.

All fishermen in Alaska owe a great deal in particular to the sockeyes, or red salmon. Why? Because it's *the sock*eyes that enter in such numbers that all other indigenous fish species drop whatever it was they were doing, pick up the scent, and begin tracking the hundreds of thousands of sockeyes, and commence feeding on the loose, drifting, pink and peach-colored salmon eggs. Sometimes these followings can extend for literally hundreds of miles, one example being the Iliamna rainbow that was caught and released at a high mountain stream a full 125 miles away from where it had been tagg*ed and released at t*he mouth of Lake IliamNA BY ALASKA FISH & Game Officials less than a week previously. All of Alaska's other sport fish species, including arctic grayling, lake trout, Dolly Varden char, and arctic char are highly effected by the annual arrival of the sockeyes.

Here's what selecting an Alaska Combination Fishing Lodge finally boils down to:

(1) It's possible that the angler may get into a situation *where* four, five, or even six Alaska sport fish species are available at any one time. But remember, any lodge providing four or *more fis*h species is doing a superb job of providing fishing opportunities.

(2) Plan your Alaska fishing trip around one specific, single fish specie and consider any and all other fishing opportunities as 'frosting on the cake' or 'gravy.'

(3) Remember, timing the salmon runs is everything. Top quality lodges are often booked-up far ahead of time, sometimes years in advance. Ask any lodge/ s you might be considering about their best dates for the specie/s you are desiring, but be ready to delay your trip for a year or so if you wish to optimize seasonal or salmon fishing conditions. Most quality lodges will be entirely honest about which species are best found at particular times.

Before scheduling your Alaska fishing trip of a lifetime realize that many lodges fly guests out to varying rivers and lakes during the course of a week's stay. If the lodge you are considering spends most of it's time fishing one particular river (and doesn't utilize floatplanes in it's daily itinerary) be cautious that that river can live up to your expectations. Always read between the lines of any advertisements you may come across - and always, ask for, and obtain referrals before booking your Alaska trip.

PIONEER LODGES

S ome of the individuals that astound me most in Alaska are the fishing lodge owners - those gambling romantics who, for one reason or another ("it certainly can't be for the money" they say) opt to brave the elements, and risk everything to build and operate an Alaska fishing lodge.

Some of the individuals that come to mind are, Raymond Petersen, Sr. and John Walatka, who teamed to build wondrous Brooks Lodge and the other, 'Angler's Paradise' lodges Katmailand still offers, along with Ray Losche of *Rainbow King Lodge*, and Ted and Mary Gerken, owners and operators of famed *Iliaska Lodge*, Iliamna's first fly-fishing-only operation. Both Losche and Gerken were "pioneers" in the Iliamna area, just as Johnny Walatka and Ray Petersen, Sr. were, years earlier, at Katmai.

On a couple of occasions I've wondered what it was like years ago, when Ted and Mary Gerken first arrived to live full-time at Iliamna. Day-in, day-out, winter and summer, come hell or high water, come freeze or thaw, winds or no winds. If I'm not mistaken, twenty years ago Iliaska was little more than a dilapidated airplane hanger and some small, scattered buildings located here and there. Come to think of it, maybe there was an old, 'roadhouse' of sorts - badly in need of refurbishing and repairs.

Quite the opposite of what Ted and Mary have turned *Iliaska* into today.

Still, it's difficult to imagine the amount of work that has gone into lodges like these, especially considering the distance involved and the efforts required just in shipping parts and supplies to the Iliamna area of Alaska. More than anything, I respect 'Alaska's Pioneers' for surviving those first few winters, Alaska can be as dark, windy, and forbidding in the winter as it can be breathtakingly beautiful in the summertime.

Fortunately, however, the pioneering spirit continues to dwell in the hearts of

173

many, especially those romantics, the would-be lodge owners here in The Great Land. God bless 'em I say,... *and here's to your Good Fortune.* Alaska needs more like you.

Just the other day I had lunch with friend, Greg Hamm, who is now readying for this coming summer season and the chance to build his own 'lodge adventure' near Iliamna. I made our lunch meeting an opportunity to introduce Greg to Tom Bukowski, who just this past year completed a small, modern lodge building of his own at Iliamna. Tom is calling his operation, "Wild Rivers," while Greg hasn't decided on a name for his lodge, yet. It was interesting for me to learn that, last year, while Tom was building his lodge, nearly 45% of his overall expenses went solely to shipping and air freight.

"I'll have a million dollar lodge, please, ...ahr, on second thought, better make that a two million dollar lodge!"

Monte Handy, who owns and operates *Last Frontier Lodge* on the Naknek River upstream from King Salmon, Alaska, is another of Alaska's romantics who has apparently decided to 'go for broke' and join the lodge owner's crowd. Apparently Monte used to own and operate an air-taxi service out of Naknek, Alaska and King Salmon that was, as far as I've been able to determine, a very successful operation. Through that experience, Monte became very knowledgeable about Alaska's best fisheries. Now, Monte has sold his airplanes, built a lodge and bought a riverboat and entered the lodge/guiding business. Apparently he's joined the throngs 'that have their hand full' juggling the multiple challenges lodge owners face - not the least of which is *praying* that weather permits them to carry out their dreams of guiding clients to some of Alaska's premier fishing, provided they have some clients to guide in the first place.

I've got a sneaking suspicion that if Monte Handy can make it through one or two more seasons he's finally got his lodge 'over the hump,' as they say. There seems to be an unwritten rule, similar to Murphy's Law, which states, "..if you can make it through your first two or three years you've got 'er made!" Mother Nature usually takes care of the rest.

Recently I learned through the grapevine that Monte Handy has booked a large group of visitors for this coming summer season (five weeks of solid visitors).

Can you imagine what it would actually be like to pull-up stakes, look the wife and kids right in the eye with a sober face and say, "....Well, I've thought things over... and....*We're going into The Lodge and Guiding Business!"*

Sounds exciting and scarry... all at the same time. It also sounds like someone might just want to go out and make friends with the local banker in a real hurry, too.

The more one learns about the dynamics of the fishing lodge business in Alaska, the more one is likely to stand in 'awe' that any fishing lodges actually 'weather all the storms they do' and stay in business in the first place. And, Mother Nature can have a lot to do with success, also.

Can you imagine all the expenses involved just in keeping the fleet floatplanes ship shape? Maybe we should ask Craig Ketchum about that subject. And, from what I hear, they don't give those airplanes away, either.

I'm really looking forward to visiting a couple of Alaska's new fishing lodges this coming season. Can't wait to get a peek at Tom Bukowski's 'Wild Rivers' at Iliamna. Tom tells me he's got 'city power,' 'city water,' and even an automatic dishwasher and a *trashmasher* - of all things. Tom says the place is insulated nicely, too. I already know how close his lodge sits to the marvelous Newhalen River, one of my favorite waters, not to mention what streams are waiting just a hop, skip, and a jump away from Iliamna.

Over at the Iliamna 'Airport Hotel,' Lem and Anesia Batchelder are beginning operations, too. Lem just bought the place from 'ol John a year or so ago, and now he's renovating the old building and making it nice and comfortable. He's even built a comfortable, new 'commons' rooms with large windows for relaxing and viewing after a hard day's fishing. Greg Niesen and Andy Macleod and I flew over and stopped in for breakfast the other day just to check things out for the opener of fishing season in a few weeks. Lem took the opportunity of showing us around a bit. I was impressed, and now that I know there's a place right next to the Newhalen where I can obtain good food, clean sheets, and good friends, I know where I'll be spending more than a few of my days this coming summer.

That's IF I can get away from the city one of these days...

Kinda makes you want to get weathered in for a few extra days, doesn't it?

So, here's to the Greg Hamms, the Monte Handys, the Tom Bukowskis and the Lem Batchelers out there who've dared to brave Alaska's elements (including the financial ones) and go ahead and build their lodges...inspite of the odds. May the fishing gods speed anglers in droves to your doorsteps, and put smiles on their faces while they spend time under your roofs.

As far as I'm concerned, there just isn't a better barometer to this place they call 'Alaska' than these 'Pioneer types' who've dropped whatever it was they were doing back in the city, looked the wife squarely in the eye, and said...

"Hold on, Honey! We're going into the lodge and guiding business!"

> **"About the time an individual gives
> up dreaming is about the same
> time that individual gives up."**
> *Anonymous*

: Mississippi.

After all, one of the joys of fishin' Alaska is building your own personal ertoire of Dream Streams...is it not?

Obtaining a good topographical map of Alaska is great advice. I've got one that I've been making notes on for years. It's all marked up with various colors of felt-tip markers, but it's led me to some of the best streams in The Greatland, and it serves to remind me of those I still need to get to know. Ironically, some of the names of the rivers on 'My Alaska Map' are the very names I couldn't even pronounce a few years ago.

As you begin to develop your own personal map, you'll begin to notice those lesser-known rivers that form integral parts of the drainages to the major river systems. By observing your map closely, you'll be able to fairly visualize the surrounding terrains of these lesser streams, and you'll also be able to determine their distances from Alaska's notable lodges or bush communities. Such information now becomes extremely valuable, because now you can begin to devise different means of arriving at the Dream Streams of your dreams via different means, depending upon the thickness of your wallet.

Sportsman's reminder: "The *Real* Alaska Begins 1/2 Hour by bush plane Outside of Anchorage".

Another wise idea would be to form a mental picture of which areas of Alaska exist as good regions for certain species you might be interested in pursuing. For example, my main fish species of interest is Alaska's rainbow trout, so now, anytime I look at a map of Alaska I am able to tell, almost immediately, which areas might fall in "rainbow territory" and which do not.

Before you know it you'll have developed a comprehensive, personal knowledge of prime waters that you'll want to investigate. As time allows you to explore them, you'll come to learn those that appeal to you most, and those which don't.

Quite possibly you'll want to begin creating your own personal list of Alaska *Dream Waters*. In one way it would be nice if there was such a thing as an 'official list of Alaska's Top Ten rivers' for each fish spices, but there are simply too many good rivers of too many varying sizes and descriptions to please everyone's expectations. Come to think of it, it might get a little crowded with everyone going to one river...

Fortunately, all fly fisher's have a way of seeking-out their own favorite 'havens.' It reminds me of the analogy of the Blind Men and The Elephant: All of the blind men felt the huge animal and 'saw' things very differently. All were 'certain' they knew and understood the elephant's real characteristics, yet in the end, they all disagreed.

Since half of the fun of fly fishing is seeking-out a few new 'fishing spots' of your own, exploring new waters in Alaska makes for exceptional adventure. Just thinking about some of the new rivers I'll be tasting and the travel and fishing opportunities this coming season gets my adrenaline flowing.

Remember, Alaska's waters *are* destroyable, so remember to do yourself — and your favorite rivers a favor— by releasing fish and not blaspheming their maiden names to Federal Union 7569 and their brothers. After all, Alaska's

FOR ADDITIONAL INFORMATION
ABOUT ALASKA'S FLY FISHING

W hether you are planning your first trip to Alaska this year or you will be returning for a second, or even a third or fourth visit, it's likely that you'll have some questions that remain unanswered. Often, anglers are unsure of which lodge, camp, or fishery is the 'correct' choice for their personal needs.

Remember, there is little purpose in booking a trip with a lodge or guide that you HOPE turns out to be the right choice. Chances are good you'll discover something other than your Alaska Dream trip - unless you know the differences between the alternative choices before hand.

It might be time that you speak personally with someone who has experienced Alaska firsthand. Should you desire additional details regarding an Alaska fishing trip, please write the following address:

FISHING ALASKA
1013 EAST DIMOND BLVD. #100
ANCHORAGE, ALASKA 99515

Be sure to include you name, address, and telephone number (including area code) in your correspondence. After your letter is received, your question/s will be assessed, and a timely response will follow, depending on the nature of your question/s. You will be contacted - and recommendations will be made to satisfy your inquiry.

Congratulations on your decision to experience Alaska's great fishing. I sincerely hope your Alaska adventure turns out to be the 'trip of a lifetime' you've always wanted.

Remember, Alaska's rivers and lodges come in many variations, sizes, and configurations, so begin your investigations months in advance of actually booking your trip.

Best of luck in your travels in....*Alaska!*

181